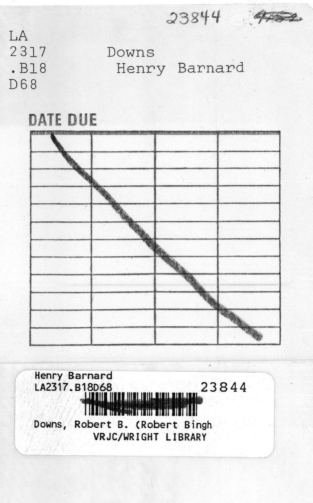

TWAYNE'S WORLD LEADERS SERIES

EDITOR OF THIS VOLUME

Samuel Smith, Ph. D.

Henry Barnard

TWLS 59

Engraved by H.W. Smith

Henry Barnard

HENRY BARNARD

By ROBERT B. DOWNS

TWAYNE PUBLISHERS
A DIVISION OF G. K. HALL & CO., BOSTON

Library of Congress Cataloging in Publication Data

Downs, Robert Bingham, 1903–
    Henry Barnard.

    (Twayne's world leaders series ; TWLS 59)
    Bibliography: p. 133–35.
    Includes index.
    1.   Barnard, Henry, 1811–1900.   2.   Educators —
United States — Biography.
LA2317.B18D68   370'.92'4   [B]   77–1775
ISBN   0–8057–7710–5

Contents

About the Author

Robert B. Downs has directed three major university libraries: University of North Carolina, 1932-38, New York University, 1938-43, and the University of Illinois, 1943-71. As Dean of Library Administration at Illinois, he served as head of the University Library and of the Graduate School of Library Science.

Dean Downs has held numerous foreign assignments, under governmental and foundation sponsorship, in Japan, Mexico, Turkey, Afghanistan, Tunisia, Sweden, Canada, the United Kingdom, and various South American countries, to establish libraries and library schools, to survey library resources and library education, and as special lecturer. He has served as First Vice President and President of the American Library Association, and President of the Association of College and Research Libraries. He holds honorary degrees from six institutions: Colby College, the University of North Carolina, the University of Toledo, Ohio State University, Southern Illinois University, and the University of Illinois.

Among other honors, Dean Downs has received the Clarence Day Award, sponsored by the Association of American Publishers, in recognition of "substantial published work promoting a love of reading"; the Joseph W. Lippincott Award "for distinguished service in the profession of librarianship"; the Illinois Library Association's "Librarian of the Year Award"; Syracuse University's Centennial Medal; and a Guggenheim Foundation Fellowship.

Dean Downs is the author of numerous books and articles, including *Books That Changed the World* (translated into 12 languages), *Books That Changed America, Famous American Books, Molders of the Modern Mind, Famous Books Ancient and Medieval, Famous Books: Great Writings in the History of Civilization,* and *Horace Mann* and *Heinrich Pestalozzi* (both in Twayne's World Leaders Series).

Preface

The roots of modern American education were planted in the mid-nineteenth century in New England by two remarkable leaders: Henry Barnard and Horace Mann. Both, in turn, had been inspired by their travels abroad and observation of European developments, particularly Heinrich Pestalozzi's Swiss schools and the work of German educators who carried on the Pestalozzian tradition.

Neither Barnard nor Mann had planned educational careers. Both were trained in law and expected to follow the legal profession. They were catapulted into the field of education almost simultaneously in the late 1830s by new legislation in Connecticut and Massachusetts establishing state boards of education — laws which they, as legislative members, had played key roles in enacting. Each was elected to, and reluctantly accepted, the secretaryship of his state's school commission. Once embarked on that track, however, they never turned back.

Barnard and Mann became ardent crusaders for public education and their influence soon spread far beyond the borders of their native states. Of the two, Mann was more colorful and controversial, but each was equally effective in his way in bringing about widespread improvements and reforms in the common school systems. Their prolific writings also had immediate and long-range significance. Today, there is an inclination to low-rate the importance of annual reports; at least in the cases of Horace Mann in Massachusetts and Henry Barnard in Connecticut and Rhode Island, however, the facts and opinions presented through this medium were widely read and had a powerful impact.

According to another comparison — length of service to the educational world — Horace Mann's career was relatively short, terminating with his death in 1859 at the age of sixty-three, while Barnard continued on until nearly ninety, though less actively in his later years.

Acknowledgement should be made to the Watkinson Library, Trinity College, Hartford, and to the New York University Library, Washington Square, New York City, for granting access to their important collections of Barnard papers.

Much appreciation should also be expressed to Elizabeth C. Downs for her assistance in research for this work, and to Clarabelle Gunning and Deloris Holiman for their assistance in the preparation of the manuscript.

ROBERT B. DOWNS

Chronology

1811	Born January 24, at Harford, Connecticut. Son of Chauncey and Elizabeth (Andrus) Barnard.
1823–1824	Student at Monson Academy, Monson, Massachusetts, and Hopkins Grammar School, New Haven.
1826–1830	Student at Yale University, graduating in 1830 with bachelor of arts degree.
1830–1831	Teaches at Wellsboro Academy, Wellsboro, Pennsylvania.
1831–1835	Reads law. Admitted to Connecticut bar in 1835.
1835–1836	Travels in Europe: England, Scotland, Ireland, Germany, Italy, and Switzerland.
1837–1839	Elected member of Connecticut state legislature.
1838–1842	Secretary of Connecticut Board of Commissioners of Common Schools. Editor, *Connecticut Common School Journal.*
1843–1849	State Superintendent of Schools in Rhode Island, and Editor of the *Journal of the Rhode Island Institute of Instruction,* 1845–49.
1847	Marries Josephine Desnoyers of Detroit.
1850–1855	State Superintendent of Schools in Connecticut, and Principal, New Britain Normal School.
1855–1881	Founder and Editor of *The American Journal of Education.* Compiler of 52 volumes of *Library of Education.*
1859–1861	Chancellor, University of Wisconsin.
1866–1867	President of St. Johns College, Annapolis, Maryland.

1867–
1870   First U.S. Commissioner of Education.

1900   Dies, Hartford, Connecticut, July 5.

CHAPTER 1

Beginning Years

A MERICAN education at the opening of the nineteenth century
has been described as in a state of bankruptcy. The nation was
preoccupied with constitutional struggles, westward expansion, the
growth of infant industries, the disestablishment of any state religion, and later the bitter controversies that culminated in the Civil
War. Throughout the colonial period and into the early decades of
the nineteenth century, education was chiefly the concern of organized religion and philanthropic individuals. American politics and
society were dominated by a laissez-faire philosophy. Questions of
educational policy inevitably became entangled with political in-
trigues, sectional jealousies, neighborhood and personal prejudices. The concept of education as a public function had to contend
with the turmoil of state and local politics and the resistance of
social inertia. As late as 1844, a friend of education in Minnesota
wrote to Henry Barnard: "The Whigs in this state are *bitter* ene-
mies of all taxation for the tuition of the children of the poor."[1] In
1850, G. F. Nagoun, an educational leader in Illinois, in another
letter to Barnard, stated that "Public education is stigmatized as a
'Yankee Notion' and men sneer at the idea of its universal
diffusion."[2]

But in the midst of all the prevailing ferment and confusion, enlightened forces were at work. Directly or indirectly, strong European influences were being exerted to inspire an American educational renaissance. Spurred on by Pestalozzi and his disciples, a
movement for popular education had developed in Prussia and
other German states and spread through the Continent. Concomi-
tantly, there developed an extensive body of literature, embodying
the writings of Rousseau, Pestalozzi, and other educational
reformers.

11

American travelers abroad brought back to their native country strong convictions about the merits of the new doctrines. Thomas Jefferson and Joseph Cabell of Virginia had become acquainted, during their residencies in Europe, with the university life of the Continent, and Cabell had visited Pestalozzi's schools. In 1817, Judge Archibald D. Murphey of North Carolina presented to his state legislature an elaborate system of popular education, based on his studies and observations in Europe and the United States. Joseph Neef introduced Pestalozzian methods into schools in Pennsylvania, Kentucky, and Indiana. Emma Willard, pioneer in the field of higher education for women, traveled abroad and returned home with advanced methods for the education of girls. The Ohio legislature sent Calvin Stowe to Germany to investigate the educational system; the published report of his findings was widely printed and reprinted for distribution in the states. Another influential voice was that of Alexander Bache, eminent scientist, who reported on methods of educating orphans, and on the elementary and secondary school systems of Great Britain and the Continental countries.

At this crucial state, the most acute need was for educational leaders who could take over and persuade the people at large that education should be a public enterprise. The country was fortunate to have a number of such far-seeing men — nearly every state had one or more. Two stand out above all the rest: Horace Mann of Massachusetts and Henry Barnard of Connecticut, contemporaries and frequent collaborators with each other, and both seasoned European travelers.

Henry Barnard was a native of Hartford Connecticut, born January 24, 1811, in a house which remained his home until his death nearly ninety years later. At the time, Hartford, though the state capital, had a population of only six thousand. The Congregational Church was still the dominant religious institution. Industry was almost nonexistent. Henry's father was a well-to-do farmer, who had also spent some time in seafaring. The boy's upbringing was mainly in his father's hands; he was only four years of age when his mother died.

Young Barnard began his education in Miss Benton's Dame

School, from which he soon transferred to the South District School. In later years, Barnard referred to himself as "a victim of a miserable district school" and stated he spent half of his life in outgrowing the bad methods of study formed there.[3] Nevertheless, the school left a permanent impress upon his mind. "It was a common school, a school of equal rights," he wrote, "where merit and not social position was the acknowledged basis of distinction, and, therefore, the fittest seminary to give the schooling essential to an American citizen."[4] With all of its deficiencies, Barnard caught a glimpse of the potentialities of a good public school.

From one of his voyages, Henry's father had brought back to Henry an orange, a truly exotic fruit at the time. His biographer, Ralph C. Jenkins, remarks that "the orange stood for many things to the boy — strange and distant lands, the exotic lure of wandering, the idea of the sea as a familiar mode of travel, and the teasing presence in the world of unknown things which he wanted to know."[5] While under this spell, Henry and a young friend, both aged twelve, resolved to run away to sea. Henry's father got wind of their plan and suggested that, instead, he transfer to the Academy at Monson, Massachusetts. The change proved to be exactly what Henry needed. As he reported later, in Monson Academy he enjoyed:

one year of thorough training in my English studies and of kind, encouraging advice as how to study and use books from that accomplished teacher, Samuel B. Woolworth, afterward principal of Cortland Academy, New York, and for a quarter of a century secretary of the board of regents of the University of the State of New York. Not less profitable was my classical instruction from the principal, Rev. Simeon Colton [one time president of Mississippi College].[6]

While at Monson, Henry began to acquire a passion for books, and to satisfy an insatiable thirst for reading and knowledge, he started to build a library which eventually reached 10,000 volumes. At this early stage, too, he started to map out a course of training which he anticipated would prepare him for a public career. His idealism is reflected in a statement written as a mature man: "Ever since I was conscious of any purpose, the aim of my life has been to gather and disseminate knowledge, useful knowledge — knowledge not always available by the many but useful to all, to gather it from sources not always available even to students and scatter it abroad."[7]

As further preparation for admission to Yale College, his chief goal at the time, Henry studied advanced Greek and surveying under a remarkable tutor, Abel Flint, and spent another profitable year in the famous old Hopkins Grammar School at New Haven. By 1826, at the age of fifteen, Barnard was ready to enter Yale.

Barnard proved himself an outstanding student at Yale. He was the best-read man of his class. Noah Porter, later Yale's president, wrote that "few professed scholars among us were so thoroughly familiar with the ancient and modern English literature as Barnard."[8] During his four years in New Haven, Barnard won prizes in English and Latin, the Berkeley prize for oratory, and was elected a member of Phi Beta Kappa — all in competition with a group of students who later produced notable judges, state governors, U.S. senators, college presidents and professors, ministers to foreign countries, and other distinguished figures. Barnard became a ready, polished, and vigorous speaker. To gain access to many books, he secured an appointment as librarian of the Linonian Society. Though he gained much from the regulation classical and mathematical courses, he commented in later life that "he owed more of his usefulness in public life to the free commingling of members of different classes, of varied tastes, talents, and characters, to the excitement and incentive of the weekly debates, to the generous conflict of mind with mind and to the preparation for the discussions and decisions of the literary societies with which he was connected" than to any other source.[9]

That Barnard was not a paragon of correct behavior was demonstrated by his participation in the "Bread and Butter Rebellion" at Yale, a student uprising to protest against the poor quality of the food being served in the college commons. For his part in the rebellion, he was sent home for a time.

While home on a visit, Barnard had long talks with the family physician, Dr. Eli Todd. From Dr. Todd, "a man of rare genius," he heard much about Heinrich Pestalozzi. Todd had met William McClure, "the first real Pestalozzian in America." From the high opinion of the Swiss educator held by McClure and passed on to Todd, Barnard became thoroughly imbued with the Pestalozzian theory of ruling by love, and his future thinking on educational matters was permanently influenced.

Following his graduation from Yale in 1830, Barnard decided to begin reading for a legal career. He was persuaded, however, by President Jeremiah Day, who had been his "guide, philosopher, and friend" during his four years at Yale, to interrupt the law training to take charge of the Wellsboro Academy at Wellsboro, Pennsylvania, in order to gain teaching experience. One year in that position gave Barnard an opportunity to study his theories of education. He appears to have pleased the school's Board of Trustees, whose letter of commendation read: "This may certify that Mr. Henry Barnard, a graduate of Yale College, has taught the Academy in this place the winter past; that as a teacher he has given universal satisfaction both to the Trustees of the Academy and his pupils, who have made rapid progress under his instruction; that he is a man of superior talents and acquirements, and of that kind which eminently qualify him for an instructor, and of good moral character."[10] But young Henry did not enjoy teaching; the Academy "reminded him of a New England common school," the district school in which he had been so miserable.

After his brief fling at public school teaching, Barnard returned to his legal studies. He read law with Willis Hall of New York and William H. Hungerford of Hartford and in 1833–34 studied in the Yale Law School. At the age of twenty-four, in 1835, he was admitted to the bar. His time had by no means been limited to his legal education, however, during the five years following his graduation from Yale. He read extensively in classical and English literature; extended travels took him through the South and West and on walking tours in Europe, covering large portions of England, Scotland, and Switzerland; and he became active in politics, spending time in Washington, where he made the acquaintance of Daniel Webster, John C. Calhoun, James Madison, and John Marshall, and listened to constitutional debates.

While Barnard was thinking over his future career, a decision
was made for him by the voters of his Connecticut district. He was
elected, without campaigning, to the General Assembly. Barnard
already had a reputation as a public speaker and was a recognized
spokesman for the young Whigs. Among the qualities fitting him
for his new office, Horace Mann pointed out, were "fine powers of
oratory, wielding a ready and able pen, animated by a generous and
indomitable spirit, willing to spend and be spent in the cause of
benevolence and humanity."[11] But offended by his youthful
appearance, the Speaker of the House thought it his duty to discipline a constituency which sent a mere lad of twenty-six to a seat
among the lawmakers of the state; consequently, the new member
from Hartford, during his first year, was completely ignored in the
appointment of standing committees. Nevertheless, Barnard's
Hartford constituency reelected him in 1838 and 1839. Barnard's
chief concern as a legislator was with humanitarian bills and resolutions. The record shows that he was involved with measures for
the education of the deaf and blind, the completion of the state
geological survey, the amelioration of the condition of paupers and
the poor, the care of the insane, the improvement of jails (including
a bill to make labor an element in all jail and prison discipline), the
incorporation of public libraries, and the rehabilitation of the Connecticut Historical Society. He opposed an attack on judicial tenure, a proposed amendment to the state constitution limiting the
tenure of office of judges to the supreme and superior courts.

The field of public education, however, became Barnard's primary interest. The *Connecticut Common School Journal* commented: "The most signal service rendered by him in the State was
in organizing and carrying through both Houses of the Legislature
in 1838, with unprecedented unanimity, an 'Act to provide for the
better supervision of the common schools', the commencement of a
new era in our school history."[12] By this act the office of Secretary
of the Board of Commissioners of Common Schools or State
Superintendent of Public Instruction of Connecticut was created.
The bill as drawn gave the Board no duties except to investigate, report and recommend, with authority to select an executive secretary
at a stipulated per diem salary. An eloquent speech by Barnard,

presenting the proposed measure, described the state of public education in Connecticut:

Our district school had sunk into a deplorable state of inefficiency and no longer deserved the name of common in its best sense, that there was not one educated family in a hundred that relied on the district school for the instruction of their children, and if they did go, the instruction was of the most elementary character. All the higher education of the State was given in denominational academies and irresponsible private schools of every degree of demerit.[13]

The Board, duly appointed by Governor William W. Ellsworth, was composed of ten members, one of whom was of course Henry Barnard. When the Board met and organized, Barnard secured the election of the Rev. Thomas H. Gallaudet as the best qualified person for secretary. When Gallaudet and a second nominee, Judge Loren P. Waldo, refused the appointment, Barnard was prevailed upon by his fellow members to accept the position for six months, and without pay. Thus did Henry Barnard forsake a promising legal and political career to devote the remaining sixty-two years of his life to the cause of public education. As a matter of fact, he had no great taste for law or politics, and was by nature best fitted to be an evangelist for popular education.

CHAPTER 2

Renaissance in Connecticut

W HEN Thomas H. Gallaudet declined to accept the newly created position of secretary of the Connecticut Board of Commissioners of Common Schools, he expressed the belief that someone with "more of the youthful strength and enthusiasm" than he possessed was required for the demanding assignment. Henry Barnard, at the age of twenty-seven, had those qualities in abundance. His reluctance to accept the secretaryship in the first place was based on two factors: he had been offered an attractive partnership by Willis Hall, then New York attorney general, and was set to begin the practice of law; and further, he had ethical scruples about taking office under a statute which he had been instrumental in passing. For the latter reason, he had insisted on a short-term appointment, without salary.

As previously noted, the secretary's duties, as prescribed by the Board, were broad in scope. They were "(1) to ascertain by personal inspection of the schools and by written communications of school officers and others, the actual condition thereof; (2) to prepare an abstract of such information for the use of the Board and the Legislature, with plans and suggestions for the better organization and administration of the school system; (3) to attend and address at least one meeting of such parents, teachers, and school officers, as were disposed to come together on public notice, in each county, and as many local meetings as other duties would allow; (4) to edit and superintend the publication of a journal devoted exclusively to the promotion of common school education; and (5) to increase in any practical way the interest and intelligence of the community in relation to the whole subject of popular education."[1]

The first act of the energetic young secretary in his new office was to draw up an elaborate address to the people of Connecticut and have it signed by all members of the Board. Tactfully phrased, the proposal was to undertake a comprehensive study of the Connecticut schools. "Connecticut ought to know the actual condition of her common schools," declared Barnard. "It is due to her dignity and her welfare to know it. But she cannot know this, without a faithful inquiry into the state of her schools. Facts are what we want," the statement continued, "and the sooner we can procure them, the sooner we shall be able to carry forward with efficiency and increased success our system of common school instruction."[2]

Following up on this communication, Barnard threw himself wholeheartedly into the task of gathering all available facts on the educational situation, using questionnaires, visits throughout the state, and personal interviews. The discouraging results were published in the Board's first report to the Legislature in 1839. It was the first thorough and reliable revelation of the actual condition of their public schools to be presented to the citizens of Connecticut. Chancellor Kent of New York, in his *Commentaries of American Law,* characterized the report as "a bold and startling document, founded on the most painstaking and critical inquiry and contains a minute, accurate, comprehensive, and instructive exhibition of the practical conditions and operations of the common-school system of education."[3]

Among the depressing facts brought to the surface by Barnard's report were these: more than half of the 1,200 schoolhouses were found to be practically unfit for occupation; large numbers of them were in incredible condition. Two hundred varieties of schoolbooks "made confusion worse confounded." Lacking enforcement of a compulsory attendance law, children went to school or not, as they chose. Only 42,000 of 67,000 children between the ages of four and sixteen were in regular attendance, and at least 8,000 attended no school whatever. The fees paid by better class families for the 12,000 children enrolled in private schools and academies totaled more than the entire sum expended on the remaining 55,000 children. Men received $15 per month for teaching in winter and women $6 to $8 per month for teaching in the summer. The length of the school term depended on the salary of the teacher. Schools were often closed in winter for lack of firewood — a strange situation in heavily-wooded Connecticut. There was no attempt at grading of schools; instead children of all ages were placed in charge of one teacher. There were no uniformity of teaching, no examination of teachers, no supervision. No county and few city districts supplemented by a local tax the regulation state appropriation of $1.25 per capita. Most discouraging of all was widespread public apathy concerning public school education, severely handicapping attempts at reform.

Barnard did not restrict himself to pointing out the faults and weaknesses of the Connecticut school system but proceeded to recommend remedies. His reports for the next three years were full of practical directions for better schoolhouses, uniformity of textbooks, supervision by the official school visitors, the just and equal division of school funds, local taxation to provide improved financial support for education, and the proper grading of schools. Great stress was placed also on providing a better qualified corps of teachers. For four years, the tireless young secretary flooded the state with reports, journal articles, circulars, and questionnaires. His days and most of his nights were devoted to the task he had undertaken. Of Barnard's four years' activity as secretary of the Board in Connecticut, Horace Mann, from the vantage point of Massachusetts, wrote:

The cold torpidity of the State soon felt the sensations of returning vitality. Its half-suspended animation began to quicken with a warmer life. Much and more valuable information was diffused. Many parents began to appreciate more adequately what it was to be a parent; teachers were awakened; associations for mutual improvement were formed; system began to supersede confusion; some salutary laws were enacted; all things gave favorable augury of a prosperous career, and it may be further affirmed that the cause was so administered as to give occasion of offense to no one. The whole movement was kept aloof from political strife. All religious men had reason to rejoice that a higher tone of moral and religious feeling was making its way into schools, without giving occasion of jealousy to the one-sided views of any denomination.[4]

An important medium of communication with teachers and others concerned with education was established by Barnard at the beginning of his tenure as secretary of the Board. The first issue of the *Connecticut Common School Journal* was published in August 1838. Its scope was as wide as the more famous *American Journal of Education,* which Barnard later edited, and in general it made for livelier reading. In the early numbers there were articles on diversity of textbooks, female teachers, the Bible in schools, newspapers, schoolhouses, infant schools, Sunday schools, school furniture, professional education, school conventions, school visitors, drawing, gravitation, reviews of educational literature, lyceums, school libraries, town associations for the improvement of schools, and schools in South America, Holland, Prussia, Michigan, Cincinnati, and New York. Later articles dealt with such topics as English school management, London schools, hygiene, the Waldenses, local history, the use of slates, normal schools, Pestalozzi, Chinese education, spelling, geography, and bookkeeping.

Financial sacrifices on Barnard's part were made to produce the *Connecticut Common School Journal,* as was the case for all his subsequent editorial ventures. Though there was a nominal subscription price of fifty cents a year for the *Journal,* a considerable number were distributed free throughout the state.

Under Barnard's guidance the Connecticut Legislature enacted a program of enlightened legislation in 1841 to strengthen the school system.

Then, suddenly, a change in the political make-up of the Legislature brought a halt to Barnard's reform program. After four years of strenuous activity, he was legislated out of office: the Board of Commissioners of Common Schools was abolished, and the progressive new school laws were repealed. The campaign that Barnard had waged inevitably encountered some opposition and disturbed local politicians. Furthermore, he had formerly been an outspoken Whig. The new Democratic governor, Chauncey F. Cleveland, in a message to the Legislature, attempted to explain the drastic action. "I think it is obvious that the public expectations, in regard to the consequence of these experiments," he asserted, "have not been realized; and that to continue them would be only to entail upon the State a useless expense. In conformity with this opinion, and in obedience to what I believe to be the public sentiment, I recommend the repeal of these laws."[5]

"Thus in the space of a day," as Ralph C. Jenkins, one of his biographers, remarked, "did Henry Barnard find himself publicly discredited, falsely accused, and dispossessed of office."[6] Another commentator, Will S. Monroe, added, "The Connecticut Legislature had blundered. Mr. Barnard had been wronged, and the schools of the commonwealth would suffer."[7]

Instead of attempting to reply to the criticisms against him, in the fourth volume of the *Common School Journal* Barnard printed in full the report of the committee which had dismissed him. In presenting it he notes, "The above report is printed with all its errors of grammar and logic, as it appears among the legislative documents of 1842."

The extent of Barnard's altruism and dedication to his task during his four-year term as secretary of the Connecticut Board is impressive. During that period, he addressed 142 public meetings and arranged 300 addresses by other educators; visited more than 400 schools in session; met with members of every school society; edited the *Common School Journal;* and paid back all his salary while expending $3,049 from his own funds. Among the movements to which he gave his support and encouragement were a law to restrict child labor in factories; lecture courses during the winter in connection with the schools; the establishment of libraries everywhere; and more generous state support for public education. Barnard's work on *School Architecture,* first published in 1839, influenced, in a practical manner, the building of better schoolhouses.

With Barnard's departure to become State Superintendent of Schools in Rhode Island in 1843, educational matters largely stagnated in Connecticut until 1849. Another political upheaval then returned the Whigs to power, and Connecticut again sought Barnard's leadership. New legislation had established a normal school at New Britain and at the same time had stipulated that its principal should also serve as State Superintendent of Education in

Connecticut. Barnard was the logical and unanimous choice for the dual position, to which he was elected on August 7, 1849. By agreement, he planned the work of the normal school but did no teaching. The immediate management of the school was placed in the hands of an assistant, T. D. P. Stone, leaving Barnard free to devote much of his time to the interests of the public schools.

Varied responsibilities were placed upon the Superintendent by the legislative act creating his office. Specific duties were to collect information from school visitors and to submit an annual report to the general assembly, including a statement of the present condition of the common schools, as well as plans for their improvement and for a better organization of the common school system; and in each county to hold a school or convention of teachers for the purpose of interesting them in the best methods of governing and teaching in the schools. The law encouraged local taxation for school support, graded schools, a reduction in the number of school officers, and a return of school management to the towns. At the time, it is reported that Connecticut had 1,650 school districts, 10,000 school officers, and 75,000 children of school age.

Though Connecticut appears to have been pleased to have its native son return home, education still held a low priority. For example, a distinguished visitor to Hartford, Thomas Rainey, editor of the *Ohio Teacher,* reported considerable difficulty in finding Barnard's office. According to Rainey's account, "after passing all the large and beautiful State offices, and then winding the long and lonesome stairs ... I landed on a dirty and unfrequented floor.... No one can imagine my astonishment and chagrin, to see the Superintendent of Public Instruction in this lonely, dark, inaccessible hole in the garret of the State House."[8] The rain poured in freely through a leaky roof during Rainey's interview.

Undeterred by physical hardships, Barnard continued his indefatigable labors. Among his concerns were parental apathy; the district system; the introduction of grades by age; public lectures and articles for the press; essays or tracts upon such topics as the history of education in Connecticut, the actual condition of schools there and comparisons with other states, school architecture, attendance and classification of children, school systems for cities and large villages, normal school textbooks and school equipment, school supervision, school support, and parental and public interest.

In Barnard's time, a majority of Connecticut's population lived in rural areas. The country schools were usually badly taught and lacked libraries and other cultural facilities available in urban centers. Among the improvements urged by Barnard were better schoolhouses, the employment of women teachers for small children during the whole year, the gathering of older children together in the winter from "a wide circuit of territory," encouragement of reading by the establishment of school libraries, and revising the course of study, so that "it should deal less with books and more with real objects in nature around, more with facts and principles which can be illustrated by references to the actual business of life"[9] — a clear reflection of Pestalozzi's influence on Barnard's ideas.

An important accomplishment of Barnard's second term as head of the Connecticut school system was a revised code of school legislation, which included all the reforms he had originally advocated. After extended discussion with teachers and the citizens of the state, followed by a debate in the general assembly, the recommended legislation was enacted in 1849. The general aims were to consolidate and to simplify the entire organization and administration of public affairs; to restore the management of the common schools to the control of the towns; to reduce the number of the too numerous school officials; to provide more equitable distribution of the state school fund; to encourage levying of local taxes to provide stronger support for the schools; and to inaugurate a graded school system.

Until this time, Barnard noted, each of 1,650 school districts was independent of all others and had only loose ties with society and the state. Of the 10,000 school officials, he added, at least 2,000 were totally incompetent, and a majority were indifferent to or neglectful of their legal obligations. As summed up by A. D. Mayo, an early Barnard biographer, the most difficult task was "to break up the obstinate Puritan conceit of local independence in public affairs under which the most important concern of the State was practically falling into the hands of little rings of officeholders.''[10]

Publication of the *Connecticut Common School Journal* was resumed by Barnard in 1852 and continued until January 1, 1855, when it was transferred to the State Teachers' Association. In the same year, 1855, Barnard began to issue the *American Journal of Education.* Another landmark in publishing was his *History of Education in Connecticut,* first brought out in 1853 as part of the Superintendent's eighth report, and in 1855 issued in a second edition; the emphasis is on the history of popular education prior to 1838, when the Board of Commissioners of Common Schools was established.

During the same period, there appeared several editions of Barnard's *School Architecture, or Contributions to the Improvement of Schoolhouses in the United States,* a widely influential work. In the fifth edition, the author dealt with: an exposition of errors in building schools; a discussion of purposes and principles in building them; descriptions of a variety of plans; illustrations of the arrangements of seats and improvements in warming and ventilation; a catalog of maps, globes, and other means of visual illustration; a list of books on education suitable for school libraries; rules for preservation of schoolhouses; and examples of exercises suitable for the dedication of schoolhouses. Of the various editions of the book, more than 100,000 copies were printed, at considerable financial loss to Barnard.

As had happened in Rhode Island, Barnard's strenuous efforts on behalf of the public schools finally exhausted his physical strength. "He drove up and down the whole of Connecticut in questionable 'buggies' pulled by even more questionable horses,'' comments Jenkins, "and at each private house of entertainment he ate flatteringly but a bit venturesomely of whatever was put before him. In New England this all too often meant pie, winter sausage, and pickles for breakfast, and the richest cakes the hostess could afford for tea.''[11] The distinguished Dr. Barnard was given the parlor bedroom, which was rarely occupied or aired, and often the windows could not be opened. A constant round of speechmaking was also physically and mentally demanding.

Thus, despite his reputedly iron constitution, Barnard's energies were spent, and in 1855 he resigned because of ill health. His successor in the superintendency was his able associate John D. Philbrick, who summed up Barnard's career to that point by asserting, "He has done more than any other man to shape the educational policy of the Nation."[12]

CHAPTER 3

Rhode Island Interlude

F OLLOWING his removal from the post of Secretary of the
Connecticut Board of Commissioners of Common Schools,
Henry Barnard began a long-cherished project to gather material
for a history of education in the United States. An extensive travel
schedule for the purpose was mapped out. A trip across the country
in 1842, in the light of still primitive travel conditions, was an
adventure in itself, demanding physical stamina and endurance.
Barnard, already an educational veteran, was only thirty-one when
his expedition began.

The route planned by Barnard took him through a number of
western and southern states. He left Hartford in October 1842 for
Buffalo and then in succession visited Cleveland, Detroit, Columbus, Cincinnati, Lexington, Frankfort, Louisville, Nashville,
Vicksburg, Jackson, Natchez, and New Orleans. Turning north
again, he made stops in Athens, Georgia; Columbia and Charleston in South Carolina; Petersburg and Richmond in Virginia; Baltimore; Philadelphia; and New York. By the first of June 1843, the
tireless traveler was back in Hartford.

Barnard's objectives on his grand tour were to visit public
schools in session and legislatures, and to interview influential individuals holding high office. Wherever he went, he was warmly wel-
comed. Speeches were delivered in every state in the existing union
except Texas. By invitation, Barnard addressed the legislatures of
ten states. His reputation as an educational expert had preceded
him and accordingly he was consulted on the drafting of school
legislation, on the planning of school buildings, and on the progress of education at home and abroad.

Meanwhile, a certain amount of educational ferment was occurring in Rhode Island, where Horace Mann's pioneer activities in Massachusetts and Barnard's frustrated efforts in Connecticut had aroused keen interest. In October 1843, "An act to provide for ascertaining the conditions of the public schools in this State, and for the improvement and better management thereof" was passed by the Rhode Island Legislature. As specified by the statute, an agent or commissioner was to be appointed "to collect and dispense, as widely as possible, among the people, knowledge of the most successful methods of arranging the studies and conducting the education of the young, to the end that the children of the State, who should depend on common schools, may have the best education that these schools may be able to impart."[1] Barnard aided in drafting the bill, and prior to its passage he addressed the state legislature on "the conditions of a successful system of public schools."

Governor James Fenner of Rhode Island recognized that Barnard was the logical choice for the new position of commissioner, and invited him to "test the practicability of his own plans of educational reform."[2] At first, Barnard was reluctant to accept the Rhode Island superintendency, on the ground that his history of education in the United States was in progress. But Governor Fenner insisted that "it is better to make history than to write it,"[3] a persuasive argument which convinced Barnard that he should accept the opportunity. It was apparent that the entire state was willing and anxious for Barnard to put into effect the kind of program which he had already carefully devised for Connecticut. Also, the political opposition encountered in Connecticut was unlikely to thwart his plans in Rhode Island, at least at the outset.

Nevertheless, in Rhode Island Barnard was faced with certain prejudices probably unique among the states. A long tradition of religious freedom prevailed. The Quakers and Baptists who had settled Rhode Island had experienced persecution elsewhere for their beliefs, and the people not only denied that religion was a concern of the state but also interpreted the phrase that the state should exercise jurisdiction "only in civil things" to exclude the responsibility for schools from the field of governmental activity. To compel a citizen to support schools or to educate his children was held to be a violation of his civil rights and freedom of conscience. Thus, there was little precedent in Rhode Island for state control of public schools, and until 1828 no public schools existed outside Providence.

Further, Rhode Island, unlike Connecticut and other states, had no public lands either inside or outside her borders, and whatever funds were appropriated had to be raised by direct taxation. Barnard's task was begun with the influential and educated citizens of the state on his side, but winning the support and confidence of the ignorant and prejudiced in the outlying districts was another matter. The virulence of the opposition was demonstrated in a speech by a legislator who, when it was proposed that the towns should raise funds by taxation to support schools, declared that such a law could not be enforced in his district "at the point of a bayonet." Another legislator's comment was to the effect that "One might as well take a man's ox to plow his neighbor's field as to take his money to educate his neighbor's son."[4]

As a consequence of these inhospitable conditions, largely rooted in history, the state of Rhode Island's schools when Barnard assumed office was even worse than in Connecticut. There was the same evil of excessive subdivision of towns into small school districts as in the neighboring state and the same excessive variety of textbooks. Schools outside of Providence were open barely three months each year. Of the 21,000 children enrolled in the public schools, the regular attendance amounted to only 13,500. It was indeed a formidable undertaking to "revolutionize the public sentiment of the State," as Barnard was charged with doing.

In approaching his assignment, Barnard employed methods similar to those adopted in his own state. Rhode Island's leaders were persuaded that no adequate legislative program could be developed without a thorough study of existing conditions. A complete survey of the state was therefore a first priority. The aim was to ascertain local situations and their causes and then, on the basis of hard facts, arouse the people to reform them. For a year and a half, Barnard went into the most remote corners of the state to preach the advantages of education and to convince the citizens of Rhode Island's lowly position among the states in educational matters and its high rate of illiteracy. In a comparatively short time he was remarkably successful in changing popular attitudes toward public schools and in winning support for financial aid from the state and local governments for their maintenance. It has been stated that while Barnard worked in Rhode Island not a single newspaper article appeared to hamper or to interfere with school progress or to stir up "angry, political, sectarian, and personal controversy" in connection with education.

The years spent by Barnard in Rhode Island were perhaps the most concentrated of his entire career. According to his own report, made at the conclusion of his stay, he had held more than 1,100 meetings and delivered in excess of 1,500 addresses. In some instances, such as teachers' institutes, meetings lasted as long as a week. About 200 sessions of parents and teachers were held to hear lectures and discussions on improved methods of teaching. Barnard's own indefatigable labors were supplemented by experienced teachers, who were employed, he noted, "to visit particular towns and sections of the state and to converse freely with parents by the wayside and the fireside, on the condition and improvement of the district school. By these various agencies it is believed that a public meeting has been held within three miles of every home in Rhode Island."[5]

Further to spread the gospel of public education, Barnard distributed gratuitously more than 16,000 books, pamphlets, and tracts, each at least sixteen pages in length dealing with educational topics. Other sources of information for the literate were the official documents issued by the state, the *Journal* of the Rhode Island Institute of Education, organized by Barnard in 1845, and articles in the public press presenting educational subjects and accounts of the proceedings of school meetings.

An amusing device adopted by Barnard to stimulate popular interest in the schools, especially to catch the attention of the rural population in remote districts, was a kind of Parnassus on wheels, known as "Baker's Circus." W. S. Baker was a brilliant, spectacular teacher and a zealous reformer, though eccentric. A large covered wagon was procured by Baker, loaded with a dozen of his best pupils and boxes of minerals, insects, and pressed flowers, to assist in object teaching. This caravan went about the country visiting isolated spots. Wherever an audience could be assembled, Baker brought out his bell, set up his blackboard, and held a school session. The children were sent to the board to do sums, draw maps, and show actual products of foreign countries. Here was perhaps the first model school on wheels. The general atmosphere was somewhat circuslike, but Barnard was able to keep Baker's showmanship tendencies within bounds and to make excellent use of his talent for teaching.

Another unlikely publicity medium found valuable by Barnard required the cooperation of almanac publishers. As he had traveled around the state, he noted that in every kitchen there hung a *Farmer's Almanac,* which was avidly read during the long winter evenings by the farmers, their wives, and their children. Here was a universal vehicle to reach all the people. Barnard composed sixteen pages or more of educational enlightenment, written in almanac style, and had the supplement sewn into every copy of the almanacs sold in Rhode Island, a total of over 10,000 annually.

Various areas of Rhode Island's educational system were in urgent need of reform in Barnard's view. A problem which had troubled his mind for some years was the irregular attendance of children. "Of course children cannot come to school if they are sick," he declared. "And the unhealthful condition of our school buildings *makes* them sick. They freeze near the windows and they roast near the stove. We must therefore improve our buildings before we can improve attendance."[6] A farmer attending one of Barnard's meetings objected, contending that exposure was good for children; it seasoned them. Snow, rain, a bit of cold, and brisk winter winds made them healthy, he insisted, as in the case of his own grandmother, who had driven off a wild Indian carrying a tomahawk, though she was armed only with a fire shovel. Barnard retorted that if exposure to the elements could develop such physical strength, the Indian ought to have been more athletic than the grandmother.

A survey of school buildings in Rhode Island during Barnard's first year as Superintendent revealed that only 312 houses were provided for 405 schools, and of these 147 were privately owned. Some

86 of the buildings were judged "absolutely unfit for habitation"; 200 had no means of ventilation; and 270 had no clock, blackboard, or thermometer. Ever a man for direct action, Barnard instructed the school commissioners not to grant any public funds to districts whose schoolhouses were not in good condition. Speedy improvement followed, with the result that Rhode Island soon had the highest ratio of satisfactory school buildings of any state in the nation. Barnard's own work on school architecture, which went through various editions, as noted, was a key factor in the reform movement. "Old, dilapidated, repulsive, inconvenient houses have given place," Barnard reported, "to new, neat, attractive, and commodious structures in a majority of the districts."[7]

Another highly detrimental aspect of the Rhode Island educational situation was the local division into small school districts. Every little town or school district acted as though it were a free and independent republic, as far as the education of its children was concerned. The lack of a central supervising authority left educaltional affairs in a chaotic state. As a consequence of the neglect of the examination of teachers and of school visitation, unqualified teachers from other states swarmed into Rhode Island. Barnard's remedies for the situation included the promotion of cooperation among districts, the consolidation of small schools into larger units, the separation of children into grades in large districts, and supervision of the schools by prominent citizens organized into visiting committees. According to Barnard's report, "Men of prompt business habits, large views of education, and a generous public spirit, have consented to act on the school committees. Committees have studied the improvements of the day, and labored to introduce them into the schools."[8]

Discrimination on the basis of sex was conspicuous in the Rhode Island schools. Boys outnumbered girls by a ratio of four to one in the total registration of pupils. Barnard found only twelve women teachers in the state outside of Providence and a few towns. He himself was convinced, as Horace Mann was in Massachusetts, that two-thirds of the children could be better taught by women, and their employment at regulation wages would add two months to the winter school term. While Barnard was state superintendent, about a hundred primary schools, under female teachers, were opened for the first time in village districts. At the end of his tenure of office in Rhode Island, he noted that "The employment of a large number of female teachers, not only in the primary, but in the district school, in the winter as well as in the summer, has improved the discipline, the moral influence, and the manners of our public schools."[9]

Another reform inspired by Barnard was the introduction of more thorough and complete courses of study. The elementary curriculum was expanded to include music, linear drawing, composition, and mathematics, especially their practical applications in everyday life. The teaching of these and other subjects was facilitated in many schools with the addition of blackboards, globes, outline maps, and materials for object teaching, then coming into vogue. A further step toward more effective and efficient teaching urged by Barnard was uniformity of textbooks in all the schools of the same towns. During his term of office, school committees in twenty-two towns adopted uniform sets of textbooks, and through quantity purchasing, obtained them at reduced prices.

Barnard's primary emphasis on finding better prepared teachers and his activities in strengthening their training have been described elsewhere. He recognized that without well-qualified teachers, all other measures to improve the educational system were doomed to failure. The chief devices adopted to secure the desired results were the examination of prospective teachers (leading to the rejection of 125 applicants in one year); demonstration teaching, such as was being done by "Baker's Circus"; teachers' institutes held in the autumn each year; and the circulation of recommended books on the theory and practice of teaching. Barnard also conducted a kind of one-man employment agency; whenever requested, he suggested "a good teacher of high moral and literary qualifications," thus helping well-fitted candidates "in obtaining desirable situations." In Barnard's opinion, "No better service can be rendered the cause of school improvement in any town."[10]

A further essential for a strong school system stressed by Barnard was adequate financial support. Summing up the success of his efforts in that area, he found that Rhode Island's annual appropriation for the support of public schools, exclusive of capital sums voted for the construction and repair of school buildings, increased by two-thirds between 1844 and 1848. For teachers' salaries, a tax raised by the state "was nearly double the amount paid out of the General Treasury for the same purpose." Also noted was the fact that in 1846, for the first time in two hundred years, every town in Rhode Island voted and collected a school tax. Barnard's missionary spirit shines through in this statement: "in every town where the appropriation has been wisely expended, better teachers have been employed, and the length of the school term has been prolonged — thus converting a portion of the material wealth of the town into intelligence and virtue, which will hereafter diffuse happiness, create wealth, and preserve it from waste."[11]

Exhausted by his strenuous activities on behalf of the Rhode Island schools, by 1848 Barnard was on the point of nervous collapse and tendered his resignation from the position of State Superintendent of Schools. Despite his impressive accomplishments, the goals he had set for himself had been only partially realized. Progress had been made on many fronts, but if his health had permitted, Barnard would have planned to go further in such directions as drafting regulations for regular school attendance by children of all ages; establishing school and public libraries; offering a course of public lectures throughout the state, supplementary to instruction in the schools; setting up a public high school in every town, for boys and girls, with two curricula, one for pre-college preparation and the second for practical training in navigation, agriculture, manufactures, and the mechanic arts; an orphan agency to seek out proper homes where fatherless and motherless children could receive good industrial and domestic training; a reform school for juvenile delinquents and a school of industry for truant, idle, and neglected children before they became tainted with vice; and a training agency for the preparation of teachers of such special schools. All these hopes and plans for the future had to await Barnard's successors, who would perhaps be inspired by his vision and example.

Upon his retirement, the Rhode Island Legislature invited Barnard to speak to a joint session on the condition and improvement of the public schools. The *Providence Journal* reported that the address was "most eloquent and impressive, and was listened to, for nearly two hours, with almost breathless attention."[12] Later a resolution was adopted by the Senate and House of Representatives and transmitted through the Governor, reading as follows:

Resolved, unanimously, that the thanks of this General Assembly be given to the Hon. Henry Barnard, for the able, faithful, and judicious manner in which he has, for the last five years, fulfilled the duties of Commissioner of Public Schools in the State of Rhode Island.[13]

Further evidence of the respect and affection in which Barnard was held came from the teachers of the state, who, at the time of his departure in 1849, presented him with a silver pitcher and a long testimonial letter in appreciation of his services to the cause of education.

A writer in the *North American Review* for July 1848 summed up Barnard's achievements in Rhode Island in these words:

Public confidence has been secured; the two political parties are of one mind about school reform. In 1846 all the towns of the State, for the first time since the colony was planted, taxed themselves for school purposes. In three years one hundred and twenty thousand dollars have been raised for school-houses out of the city of Providence; and the traveler is now delighted at the external neatness, the internal convenience, and in some instances the architectural beauty of the school-houses that have everywhere sprung up. Teachers of a high order have been introduced; good wages are paid; and a vigilant supervision has been established.[14]

Barnard was not, of course, long to remain free of educational burdens. After a period of rest and recuperation, he was back at the helm in his native state as Superintendent of Common Schools of Connecticut.

CHAPTER 4

University President

ONE of the least happy and successful times in Henry Barnard's long educational career was the short period in which he served as chancellor of the University of Wisconsin and president of St. John's College, Annapolis, Maryland. Nevertheless, his accomplishments, especially in the former position, were of considerable significance.

His fame as an educator led several universities to offer Barnard the post of president. After considering Indiana University, the University of Michigan, and Washington University in St. Louis, he decided, in 1858, to accept the Wisconsin opening. It is probable that his decision was influenced by earlier associations with the state. As early as 1846, he had been invited to present two addresses before the Wisconsin Constitutional Convention on the subject of popular education. His scheme — embodying proposals for local taxation in connection with the distribution of the state school fund; a state superintendent of schools; and the establishment of a state university with a normal school department — was adopted in 1848. A few years later, during the summer of 1851, Barnard conducted a series of teachers' institutes in twenty or more Wisconsin counties.

Aside from some familiarity with the local scene, Wisconsin held other attractions for Barnard. The University was favorably located in a wealthy state with an intelligent and progressive population. The proportional number of children of school age was the largest of the common school states. The school fund, derived from the national gift of public lands, had reached $3,000,000 and promised to grow. There were already about twenty free high schools established in the larger towns. A dynamic state superintendent of

36

schools, Lyman C. Draper, was stimulating state-wide interest in educational affairs, through his vigorous reports and other activities.

On the other hand, the University of Wisconsin was in desperate straits. Its land had been sold for a fraction of its true value. A legislative act of 1857, restricting the sale of school and university lands, had come too late to prevent what a Joint Legislative Committee had termed "criminal negligence, wanton recklessness, and utter disregard for the most responsible duties that could be imposed on man."[1] Within five years 4,000,000 acres granted the state for school and university support had been plundered. There had been great irregularities and frauds in the sale of the lands. Furthermore, a hostile legislature refused to appropriate maintenance funds for the University, forcing the institution to borrow money to continue its operations. The numerous small colleges in the state succeeded in securing a share of the proceeds from the sale of public lands, and they waged constant warfare on the University's interests. By 1855, the situation had become so desperate that suspension of the University was seriously considered.

It was against this background that Barnard accepted the chancellorship. His appointment was greeted with enthusiasm and relief by the Board of Regents, the faculty, the educational world generally, and the public. Great expectations were aroused. Superintendent Draper expressed the prevailing sentiment in his 1857 report: "As a promoter of the cause of education, the career of Dr. Barnard has no precedent and no parallel. We have reason to felicitate ourselves on the acquirement of such a man. It ought to form a new era in our State history, and it will if we are true to ourselves and true to him."[2] The very fact of the excessive expectations and the complete confidence of the educational public was in itself a peril to Barnard's success.

In any event, he entered upon his duties with high hopes. "I like my prospective field of labor in Wisconsin," he wrote. "Madison is a charming spot and there is work enough to fill my highest expectations."[3] In a later letter, he commented, "The facilities for laying the foundations of a great work are even greater than I anticipated and in about three years time, I hope, if my health holds out, to see some fruits of my labor."[4]

In his dual capacity as Chancellor of the University and agent of the normal board of regents, Barnard was specifically charged "to visit and exercise a supervising control over the normal departments of all such institutions as shall apply for a participation in the normal school fund, to conduct teachers' institutes and normal instruction in the same, and to cooperate with the superintendent of public instruction in procuring a series of public educational addresses to be delivered in the various parts of the State."[5] The scope of his responsibilities was noted also in a letter dated July 29, 1859: "I am expected to visit every portion of a State territory as large as the whole of New England — hold twelve Teachers' Institutes in as many counties or sections — visit 15 institutions, which receive aid from the Normal Instruction Fund — and busy myself at odd intervals with many things in general and some things in particular of the University, besides assisting in reorganizing the public school of Madison and establishing a Female Seminary there."[6]

Aside from his assigned functions, Barnard had a well-conceived set of recommendations to offer the regents. He proposed that the University's preparatory department be transferred to the Madison High School; the normal department be developed; practical instruction be added in the application of science to individual and public health, to agriculture, architecture, and other industrial areas; less be spent for buildings and more for instruction; students be classified by individual studies and not by groups of studies or period of residence; and degrees be granted after a public examination. Barnard's chief objectives were to unify all the state's educational forces, from the kindergarten to the University; to make the University's influence felt in the state's educational movement; to develop the University's internal life with a view to meeting the needs of the state to raise high school standards to produce better-prepared students for the University; and to obtain legislative support for the establishment of a polytechnic department within the University. "A State cannot have good elementary schools or an efficient University," declared Barnard, "without schools of an intermediate grade, developing and encouraging a love of learning in the young, and furnishing the necessary preparation for the studies of the University. As far as I can now see, this is the weak point of the system of public instruction in Wisconsin.''[7]

Unfortunately, the precarious state of Barnard's health, the bane of his public career, prevented him from carrying the Wisconsin program to a successful conclusion. Even before assuming the duties of the new office, his inauguration as chancellor was delayed a full year, until July 27, 1859, because of severe illness. Early in 1860 he suffered an attack of "nervous prostration" and left Wisconsin in May. Barnard resigned his position during the summer, but, hopeful of a recovery, the regents did not accept his resignation until January 17, 1861.

In such a short period, broken by frequent absences, what did Barnard actually achieve for Wisconsin? Much was of an intangible nature. His primary interest in the public schools and in teacher education caused him to pay limited attention to the University and its needs and problems. Barnard had accepted the dual position in the first instance, however, with the understanding that he would be released from all instructional duties in the University in order to concentrate his attention on strengthening normal schools and teachers' institutes. Not unnaturally, University faculty members were somewhat critical and resentful at having their concerns subordinated to other educational agencies. In his defense, one of Barnard's first biographers, A. D. Mayo, states:

There is no evidence that the educational public or the people of Wisconsin were disappointed in their expectations of the value of the services of their new citizen educator. But the time of his coming was not auspicious for the cause of education. Already were the clouds thickening along the horizon that prognosticated the breaking of the awful tempest of the civil war.[8]

For the five years following his resignation, it is doubtful that Barnard would have been able to carry on his educational activities in Wisconsin, even if his health had permitted him to remain in the state. Preoccupation with the Civil War was absorbing the attention and energies of Wisconsin citizens along with those of the nation as a whole. Nevertheless, as Blair points out, "it is true that Henry Barnard entered the State at a crucial time and gave a powerful impulse to influences and ideals already at work. It cannot be said with scientific accuracy that this or that characteristic feature of the Wisconsin system today resulted from his efforts. But it can be said that the outstanding feature peculiarly characteristic of the system, its sensitive response to the needs of the State and its careful adjustment to meet them, is in harmony with the doctrine that he preached most insistently in the Public School Crusade of 1859."[9]

This evaluation and judgment was confirmed by a greeting from the president and faculty of the University of Wisconsin sent to Barnard on the occasion of his eighty-sixth birthday:

We, who have entered into the fruits of your early work, recall your enthusiastic labors in preparing the way for higher education in this State. Your sagacity early recognized that the foundations of a State university must be laid among the people, and you devoted yourself with contagious zeal to the upbuilding of the schools of this Commonwealth.[10]

It was always a matter of keen regret to Barnard that his health prevented him from directing the development of an institution destined to become one of America's great state universities.

For the next six years, Barnard held no public office, leaving him free for editorial labors on the *American Journal of Education* and other educational literature. In 1866, he was tempted to re-enter the administrative arena by the offer of the presidency of St. John's College, Annapolis, Maryland. St. John's, founded in 1784, with antecedents going back to 1704, was ostensibly to serve, along with Washington College on the Eastern Shore, as the University of Maryland. State support, however, was limited and intermittent, and the college led a precarious existence until the outbreak of the Civil War, when it closed its doors. During the war years, its buildings served as a hospital.

At the conclusion of the war, the St. John's Board of Visitors determined to reopen the college, and Barnard was invited to accept the presidency. Apparently Barnard saw in the position an opportunity to develop an integrated system for an entire state, as he had planned to do in Wisconsin. The offer was accepted, and Barnard was formally inaugurated on January 7, 1866.

In his inaugural address, Barnard projected an ambitious plan for the future of St. John's, far beyond the institution's meager financial resources. The curriculum was to be divided into eleven departments, the teaching of English and modern languages was to be emphasized, new laboratories were to be provided, and the library re-stocked.

When the college actually opened in September 1866, there was a faculty of twelve, with Barnard serving as principal and professor of mental, moral, and social science. Students were enrolled in a preparatory department and a freshman class. Barnard traveled over the state hoping to stimulate support for a strong institution. Disillusionment rapidly followed. Pleas for contributions to establish scholarships and for the acquisition of books for the library were of little practical effect. A Democratic majority in the legislature was unfriendly to the Republican Board of Visitors who had elected Barnard. There were threats that the legislative grant to St. John's would be withdrawn. At this critical juncture in the history of the college, Barnard was appointed United States Commissioner of Education and promptly resigned the presidency, after one year in office. The college had been re-established, but any expectation that it would become head of the state's system of education was frustrated by its location and political opposition. In any case, as Jenkins remarks, "a Northerner, in 1866, attempting to revive an old Southern college under a new and strange policy, with inadequate financial backing, was laboring against intolerable odds."[11]

In retrospect, it appears that Barnard lacked strong qualifications for a university or college presidency and that his interests lay elsewhere. That he recognized this weakness in himself is evidenced by a surviving statement, written in 1858: "My own experience and studies qualify me, in my own judgment, more for the work of organization and administration of a State System, shaping the professional training of teachers, and the school movements of the State generally, than for the details of college discipline and instruction, for which I have no special aptitude and no experience, and which at my time of life I have no desire to undertake."[12] It is somewhat ironical that Barnard's two ventures into the field of higher education were made after making the foregoing comment.

CHAPTER 5

National Educator

T HE need for a department of the federal government to deal with educational matters was recognized by Henry Barnard some thirty years before the actual creation of such an agency. When the Department of Education was finally approved by Congress, in good part due to Barnard's efforts, he was ambitious to become its first Commissioner. In a letter to Daniel Coit Gilman on January 10, 1867, Barnard wrote: "It is the only office under gift of government which I would turn on my heel to get, as thirty years study and action have fitted me for this work, and I should like to wind up my educational labors in inaugurating this office."[1]

The Constitution of the United States makes no mention of education. The question of including education among the powers assigned to the federal government was discussed by the Constitutional Convention at Philadelphia in 1787, but it was there decided that, though very important, education was a matter better left to the individual states. Federal interest in education subsided thereafter until 1840, when Barnard induced federal officials to add questions on literacy to the schedules for the 1840 census. The following year, on the basis of the returns, Barnard prepared an address on "The Magnitude of the Educational Interests of the United States and the Necessity of Great and Immediate Improvement in State and City Systems of Public Instruction." From that time forward, until their goal was achieved, Barnard, Horace Mann, and other leading educators actively promoted the idea of a department of education in the federal government.

In 1845 and again in 1847 Barnard attempted to get "the diffusion of a knowledge of the science and art of education, and the organization and administration of systems of public schools" into the plan of the Smithsonian Institution, at the time in process of establishment. On October 17, 1849, "a national convention of the friends of common schools" met in response to a call from Barnard, Mann, and others. One of the resolutions adopted by the meeting recommended "that a committee of five be appointed to prepare a memorial to Congress asking the establishment of a bureau in the home department for obtaining and publishing annually statistics in regard to public education in the United States."[2] There followed, in 1851, a meeting of the officers of the American Institute of Instruction, at Lynn, Massachusetts, where a committee was appointed "to consider the expediency of petitioning Congress with reference to the establishment of an educational department at Washington."

Interest in the subject continued when the American Association for the Advancement of Education, meeting in Washington on December 26, 1854, approved a resolution for the distribution of public lands in support of education and stated that "it entertains the strongest convictions that the interests of public education will be greatly advanced by the establishment in connection with one of the departments of government of a depository for the collection and exchange of works on education and the various instrumentalities of instruction."[3] Barnard's biographer A. D. Mayo wrote that "All proceedings of this body of educators . . . had but one logical tendency — that in some way the National Government should interest itself again in the education of the whole people."[4]

The Civil War interrupted for a time the accelerating movement toward a federal agency for education, though there continued to be intermittent pressure for a national bureau by such organizations as the National Teachers Association and the National Association of State and City School Superintendents. A memorial prepared by a committee appointed by the latter society was presented to Congress by James A. Garfield, then a Representative from Ohio, who at the same time introduced a bill to establish a National Bureau of Education. In the debate which followed, the bureau became a department, the bill passed both houses of Congress, and on March 2, 1867, it was signed by President Andrew Johnson. About two weeks later, on March 14, 1867, Henry Barnard became the first U.S. Commissioner of Education.

Specific functions to be carried on by the new agency were defined in the original statute as follows:

To collect statistics and facts showing the condition and progress of education in the several States and Territories, and to diffuse such information respecting the organization and management of schools and school-systems, and methods of teaching, as shall aid the people of the United States in the establishment and maintenance of efficient school-systems, and otherwise promote the cause of education throughout the country.[5]

By means of circulars to institutions and to school superintendents throughout the country, the provisions of the act establishing the department were publicized. Because of his extensive acquaintance with educational systems and institutions in America and Europe and his numerous contributions to professional literature, Barnard's name was already familiar to the nation's educators. A warm tribute came from James L. Hughes of Toronto, who wrote: "It was but fitting that the man who has done most to organize the state and city school systems of the United States, who had conducted the first County Teachers' Institute on lines similar to the present summer schools, who had championed the cause of woman by demanding for her equal educational privileges with man as a student and as a teacher, who had established the first state system of libraries, who was the first to propose a national organization of teachers, and who had published more educational literature than *any other man in the history of the world,* should be the first Commissioner of Education appointed by the government of the United States."[6]

Barnard lost no time in beginning his duties. A comprehensive inquiry was immediately instituted into the administration, instruction, and management of elementary schools, colleges, professional and special schools, societies for the advancement of education, school funds and educational endowments, legislation with respect to schools, school architecture, charitable and reformatory institutions, school documents, and memoirs of teachers and benefactors of education.

The results of Barnard's far-flung investigations were presented in an 881-page report submitted to Congress in 1868. William T. Harris, a later Commissioner, described the document as "the chief monument of Dr. Barnard's career as Commissioner of Education."[7] Its contents include a compilation of statistics relating to the states and cities of the country, followed by five appendices dealing with illiteracy in the United States, the legal status of the black population in various states, art instruction, public instruction in German cities, courses of studies in major U.S. cities, and teachers' salaries in several cities.

Perhaps because of the disturbed conditions and generally controversial atmosphere prevailing immediately following the Civil War, Barnard was in difficulties almost from the beginning in the Commissioner's position. At the outset there had been opposition to the establishment of a separate department, rather than a bureau, for education. Every appropriation bill was the signal for a battle. Arguments raged concerning federal and states' rights and on the use of coercive measures in the South. The functions of a Department of Education were not understood by Congress, and Barnard was unable to define them clearly, or at least not in terms understood by Congress. An unprincipled clerk in the Department was an informer against Barnard, for the purpose of gathering information to undermine and discredit him.

Barnard was largely defenseless in countering such tactics. In a letter to a supporter, Representative Ignatius Donnelly of Minnesota, he pointed out that he had the nearly unanimous backing of every superintendent of public schools as well as hundreds of active friends of education throughout the country, all of whom would have attested to his competence.

The odds, however, were too great. On July 20, 1868, the Department was abolished, to be replaced by an Office of Education. The salary of the Commissioner was reduced from four thousand to three thousand dollars,and the clerical staff cut back to two low-ranking clerks. In November, Secretary Jacob Cox of the Department of the Interior, designated to take over the office, submitted an annual report, in which he asserted that the Office of Commissioner had been abolished by the July 20 action and that the functions of the new Office of Education should be assigned to existing agencies. "Interference by Congress in matters of purely local concern," he declared, "can be productive of nothing but unmixed evil." Moreover, in the Secretary's opinion, an appropriation of $6,000 was ample "if the office is economically administered. No greater clerical force should be authorized."[8]

Various charges against the Commissioner were filed with the Committee on Appropriations by a clerk dismissed by Barnard. The anonymous complaints stated that the Commissioner spent too much time away from his Washington office; that government departmental documents were printed in the *American Journal of Education;* that employment of experts for special investigations was illegal; and that funds had been misappropriated. The charges were later characterized by Representative Samuel F. Cary, Chairman, in his House Report, as "either so frivolous as to be unworthy of any serious attention, or so malicious as to fail of their purpose."[9] Barnard was naturally highly indignant, summing up the situation with the statement, "All my experiences with wild beasts and stolid asses in an experience of 30 years did not lead me to expect what I am now receiving."[10]

By 1870 the end was in sight. A bill to abolish the Office was presented and debated in the House of Representatives on February 21. On March 15, after less than two years in office, the Commissioner resigned. President Grant appointed as his successor John Eaton, a retired brigadier general. Eaton was faced with the task of building up the bureau and demonstrating its value. He had administrative talent, a flair for publicity, and strong support from the President. Under his direction, the bureau's activities were concentrated thereafter on the collection and dissemination of educational information and familiarizing educators with the best educational practices at home and abroad.

From the perspective of the bureau itself, Eaton, years later, wrote an account of Barnard's association with the agency. As summarized by Commissioner Eaton, Barnard's principal contributions were these:

(1) He gave his utmost influence to the establishing of the bureau; (2) he

sought to make reports which would be truly national; (3) he sought most carefully to devise valuable forms for statistics and abbreviated statements; (4) he began the publication of circulars giving information in regard to miscellaneous educational topics; (5) he enforced the national obligation to education; (6) he emphasized the need of universal education; (7) he would make the bureau enforce the universal relation of education to all the details of man's improvement; (8) he would make it understood that the laws of education in their relation to man's welfare were the same to all races; (9) he would draw illustrations of educational processes from all nations and peoples; (10) he sought to stimulate improvement by using both the historical and comparative methods, setting over against each other different years and different institutions and systems, by the publication of facts.[11]

In autobiographical notes, written long afterward, Barnard had a single entry: "Washington — a dismal experience." The reasons for his failure in the national office, despite the notable accomplishments cited by Eaton, were complex. Anna Lou Blair, one biographer, concluded that Congress may not have been entirely to blame for the debacle. After a long career as an unquestioned authority, Barnard had become something of an educational dictator. Early in his career, he had exercised great tact and diplomacy in dealing with opposing forces in Connecticut and Rhode Island. But a quarter of a century later, he showed no patience with Congressmen who showed a similar lack of understanding and sympathy for educational progress. His inflexible determination was to carry out in his own way his plans and ideas for the newly-created national Department of Education. That frame of mind led him on a certain collision course with Congress.

The position of Commissioner of Education as visualized by Barnard was, in any case, a practically impossible assignment, given the limited resources at his command. Viewed nationally, education was in a chaotic state. Northern elementary schools had suffered severely during the Civil War, and those which had existed in the South were completely wrecked. The western states needed much aid and advice in setting up systems of public schools. For such a truly formidable task, the Commissioner was given a staff of but four (later reduced to two) and funds amounting to only about

$12,000 to cover salaries and expenses for two years.

Thus ended thirty-four years of Barnard's almost continuous official service to education. He never again accepted a public office.

CHAPTER 6

Author and Editor

H ENRY Barnard was amazingly prolific as author and editor of educational literature. From a long-range point of view, his most enduring contributions are unquestionably in that area, and Barnard himself appeared to be happier as a writer than as an educational administrator.

Educational journalism came of age in America with the appearance of Barnard's *Connecticut Common School Journal* in 1838 and Horace Mann's *Common School Journal* in 1839. Barnard's Connecticut venture was the first of two trial runs, marking the beginning of his journalistic career. As secretary of the Board of Commissioners of Common Schools, he established the *Connecticut Common School Journal,* drawing largely on his European experiences for material, plus statistical information concerning the schools of Connecticut and frank discussions of the shortcomings and strengths of the educational system. The *Journal* ran from 1838 to 1866.

Barnard continued his editorial activities following his appointment as Rhode Island's State Commissioner of Public Schools. He took the lead in the organization of the Rhode Island Institute of Instruction, one of the oldest teachers' associations in America, and, with its support, founded the *Journal of the Rhode Island Institute of Instruction,* issued from 1845 to 1849.

After these preliminary ventures, Barnard began to envision a truly national education journal. By 1854, he felt that the time was ripe and accordingly submitted an elaborate proposal to the American Association for the Advancement of Education. The plan recommended a three-part publication program: a quarterly or monthly journal of education, producing an octavo volume annually of at least 600 pages; a library of education, to consist of a series of independent treatises, covering some thirty-two subjects, "constituting when complete an encyclopedia of education"; and, finally, a comprehensive history of education in the United States, for which Barnard had already collected a large volume of material.

The American Association for the Advancement of Education lacked the financial means to back Barnard's ambitious proposal but endorsed the general plan. Undaunted, Barnard decided to proceed on his own. In the first issue of the *American Journal of Education,* Barnard wrote:

In the absence of any funds belonging to the Association, and of any pledge of pecuniary cooperation, on the part of individuals, the Standing Committee have not taken any steps to establish a central agency for the advancement of the objects for which the association was instituted, or felt authorized to provide for any publication beyond the proceedings of its last annual meeting. Under these circumstances, the undersigned has undertaken on his own responsibility, to carry out the original plan submitted by him, so far as relates to the publication both of the Journal, and the Library — relying on the annual subscription of individuals in different states, and interested in different allotments of the great field, who desire to be posted up in the current intelligence and discussion of schools and education, to meet the current expenses of the former; and on special contributions in aid of the latter, by persons or institutions interested in particular treatises, as their preparation shall be from time to time advanced and announced.[1]

The scope of the new journal, as described by Barnard in the initial number, was to be comprehensive of the entire field of education. It would "embody the matured views and varied experience of wise statesmen, educators and teachers in perfecting the organization, administration, instruction and discipline of schools, of every grade, through a succession of years, under widely varying circumstances of government, society and religion."[2] Other announced aims were to present and if possible harmonize conflicting views, point out deficiencies in education, stimulate reforms, and in general "serve as a medium of free and frequent communication between the friends of education." While Barnard proposed to deal with the history, discussion, and statistics of systems, institutions, and methods of education in different countries, he expected to pay special attention to the "condition and wants of our own."

For the next twenty-seven years, 1855 to 1882, Barnard carried on the editorship of the *American Journal of Education.* The publication of thirty-two volumes of about 800 pages each during this period consumed the greater part of his inherited fortune. In the vast bulk of material was included everything which Barnard judged was of any conceivable value to American teachers. The accumulation of educational information and biography covered nearly every phase of educational history from the earliest periods to the 1870s. The most detailed account of the history and contents of the *Journal* is presented in Richard Emmons Thursfield's study, *Henry Barnard's American Journal of Education.*[3]

History and biography occupied about one-third of the *Journal's* total space. The range was from educational systems in use under the Ptolemies in ancient Egypt down to the methods being developed for the education of the Cherokee Indians. Controversial matter, however, was omitted. For example, Barnard excluded any consideration of education for blacks as long as slavery existed and ignored the "educational" program of the temperance movement. On the other hand, while keeping the *Journal* free of sectional or partisan policies outside the field of education, controversial topics in the educational sphere were treated. Articles were published on the kindergarten, women's education, physical education, the role of the college, the nature of the university, curricular changes, agricultural education, scientific studies, the place of the classics, and other areas where unanimity of opinion was lacking. Here, too, there were limits, for Barnard would not admit current socialistic or radical educational ideas or plans to his pages. State education he regarded as a safe socialistic reform, however, for he had faith that education was the chief instrument for improving and ultimately perfecting mankind.

Barnard drew extensively for his scholarly editorial work upon his excellent private library of more than 10,000 titles, undoubtedly the most complete educational library in America. It included an unrivaled textbook collection. Because of the editor's reputation and wide acquaintance, textbooks, documents, journals, and pamphlets poured into his study from all over the country and from Europe. Many publications were received in exchange for copies of the *Journal*. Other information for the *Journal* was gathered by Barnard and his friends on trips to Europe.

From the beginning of his editorship of the *Journal* Barnard presented descriptions and histories of the different school systems in the various states and in the larger cities. Much attention was given also to educational statistics, of which Barnard had been a constant collector since his term as secretary of the Connecticut Board of Commissioners of Common Schools in the late 1830s. In his view, statistics provided a scientific approach to educational problems. Hours of labor, search, and correspondence were expended in preparing statistical tables of libraries, schools, colleges, reformatory institutions, and numerous other aspects of the educational field.

Thursfield describes the *American Journal of Education* as "an unrivaled collection of primary and secondary sources for the story of American educational development from early colonial times to about 1880."[4] Barnard's own contributions as author are of several types: original biographical-historical accounts, many brief historical articles, reprints of historical descriptions written as part of Barnard's educational reports or from his separately published books, and innumerable documents, speeches, reminiscences, and summaries. An example of his careful scholarship is the "History of Common Schools in Connecticut," which is scattered through several volumes of the *Journal,* though as Thursfield notes, "encumbered with frequent and long excerpts from original documents and published accounts."[5] The history of elementary education in other states also receives due attention but usually in the form of biographies of leaders of the common school revival, and speeches, reports, and documents.

Another topic in the forefront of Barnard's interests was teacher education in America. Since the beginning of the movement for the professional preparation of teachers in America was contemporary with Barnard, some of the accounts were written as history while still in the nature of current events. Earlier articles on the subject in the *Journal* were supplemented and updated by a historical record of normal schools, entitled "Institutions for the Professional Training of Teachers in the United States," published in 1868. Articles appeared from time to time on a related development, beginning around the start of the nineteenth century: the history of educational associations formed for the professionalization of American education.

Barnard's broad concept of education is revealed by accounts in the *Journal* of experiments in combining physical culture and manual labor with intellectual training and the early history of agricultural and mechanical education. The beneficial effects of combining physical exercise or manual labor with mental work are stressed.

Secondary and higher education is dealt with, in its various aspects, by the *Journal*. The editor or contributors wrote histories of Latin grammar schools, academies, and high schools, especially of pioneer schools in Connecticut and elsewhere in New England. There are biographies of benefactors and principals, histories of separate institutions, reminiscences of students, and statistical data. Various types of articles appeared also on American collegiate education, including histories of individual colleges and biographies of college presidents, professors, and benefactors of higher education. Enlightening discussions were included on the controversies prevalent in the mid-nineteenth century, both in the United States and Europe, on the proper form and function of higher education.

As part of the record of American education, Barnard printed in the *Journal* reminiscences concerning schools and teachers, contemporary accounts of education, and important educational documents, including some of the classics of the American public school revival. Prominent educators, former teachers, public officials, and ministers, men and women, told of schools, schoolhouses, schoolbooks, and schoolteachers as they recalled them from the late eighteenth and early nineteenth century. Among the contributors were Heman Humphrey, president of Amherst; Eliphalet Nott, for sixty-two years president of Union College; Noah Webster, eminent lexicographer; Edward Everett, Horace Bushnell,

Samuel G. Goodrich [Peter Parley], and A. Bronson Alcott.

Famous documents relating to American education reprinted in the *Journal* by Barnard included selections from Calvin Stowe's *Report on Elementary Public Instruction in Europe,*[6] Horace Mann's *Seventh Annual Report,*[7] and Barnard's own "Gradation of Public Schools with Special Reference to Cities and Large Villages."[8]

Biography was always a favorite subject with Henry Barnard, and educational biography filled a substantial portion of the *Journal,* from the first volume to the last. The editor hoped that a record of American educational leadership, past and contemporary, would be a source of encouragement and inspiration to teachers and others in the field of education. Accounts of more than 230 American educational leaders, teachers, and benefactors were prepared for and printed by the *Journal.* The series encompassed heroes of the public school movement, textbook authors, educational journalists, private school executives, normal school founders and principals, public school administrators, leaders of various phases of special education, community leaders of educational activity, college professors and presidents, leaders of educational movements, and educational philanthropists. A majority of the accounts dealt with nineteenth-century figures. Barnard was quite evidently a believer in Thomas Carlyle's great-man theory of history and was convinced that educational progress could be shaped and directed by dynamic leadership supplied by educational statesmen and devoted teachers.

Turning from the American experience, the *American Journal of Education* also brought to its readers the most complete record of foreign educational thought and experience — all in the English language. Emphasis was placed upon comparative studies in foreign education. According to one statistical analysis, discussions of foreign education, often historical, occupy one-fourth of all the *Journal's* space. German, British, and French led, in the order named; but Holland, Canada, Sardinia, Norway, Sweden, Belgium, Greece, and less important countries were represented.

Barnard believed that the basic aspects of American culture were western European in origin and he felt obligated to transmit the best of its educational literature to his readers, though recognizing at the same time the necessity for adapting the European experience to American institutions and to the American environment. An outlook that was too narrowly nationalistic or provincial, with too little knowledge of the history of education, in his view would result in time and effort being wasted rediscovering what was already known. Frequently, what novices in the field regarded as original discoveries had been conceived and tested seventy years before by Pestalozzi and his teachers and over two hundred years earlier by Comenius.

In searching for a history of European education for publication in the *Journal,* Barnard explored the rich German pedagogical literature. Two works were finally selected as the best and latest treatises on the subject: Karl von Raumer's *History of Pedagogy,* a four-volume opus; and J. H. Krause's *History of Education.* All of the third volume of Savigny's *The History of the Roman Law During the Middle Ages* was translated, and much of Karl Adolf Schmid's *Encyclopedia of Education* was taken over. Von Raumer's philosophy of education was particularly in accord with Barnard's views, with its democratic and liberal ideas, its insistence on the state's duty to provide education, and its biographical approach to history. Installments from Von Raumer's work were serialized in nine volumes of the *Journal.* The Von Raumer history drew extensively upon earlier writers, and through this source American readers were introduced to the educational teachings of Martin Luther, Comenius, Francis Bacon, Wolfgang Ratke, and others.

The first extended account of Pestalozzi and his progressive educational views in the *Journal* was a translation of Von Raumer's biographical study. Pestalozzi's great faith in education as a means of regenerating society and his humane approach were especially attractive to Barnard. The Von Raumer life was followed by published translations in the *Journal* of a number of Pestalozzi's own writings: *Evening Hours of a Hermit, Leonard and Gertrude,* and *How Gertrude Teaches Her Children.* In 1874, Barnard brought out a separate volume, *Pestalozzi and His Educational System,* in which was assembled Pestalozzian material from various issues of the *Journal.* Barnard saw Pestalozzi's ideas as offsetting the extreme materialism typical of nineteenth-century America and the prevailing emphasis on utilitarian education.

Von Raumer wrote to Barnard commending the thoroughness of coverage of the Pestalozzi compilation.[9] And Thursfield noted the congeniality of Barnard's and Pestalozzi's educational views.[10]

From a German source, Barnard picked up a regular department entitled "Educational Aphorisms and Suggestions, Ancient and Modern," including passages from the Bible, and by Confucius, Zoroaster, Pythagoras, Plato, Quintilian, and other ancient thinkers down to Goethe, Kant, and Niemeyer. Comments on schools and education from such dramatists as Aeschylus and Shakespeare, political economists Adam Smith and John Stuart Mill, literary figures Milton and Wordsworth, and from religious leaders, philosophers, statesmen, social reformers, and educators provided wide perspective and demonstrated the timeless and universal concern for education.

British sources were drawn upon almost as freely as the German by Barnard. English books, journals, pamphlets, newspapers, and documents were regularly scanned for relevant material on the history of education and comparative education. About one-half of Edward Kirkpatrick's *Historically Received Conception of the University,* for example, appeared in the *Journal,* along with selections from John Henry Newman's *Rise and Progress of Universities,* and portions of Capes' *University Life in Ancient Athens.* Classics relating to education were reprinted in their entirety or substantially so.

Other phases in the history of education in the Western world were filled in by Barnard with works chosen from France, in particular, Austria, Russia, and smaller nations. European educational biography from ancient times to the mid-nineteenth century dealt with the lives of numerous educational leaders. It is apparent that Barnard intended the *Journal* to be all-encompassing for education and its history, though the lack of information from other areas of the world limited him largely to Western Europe and the United States. In any event, Barnard clearly demonstrated his conviction that education knows no boundaries and that there should be no isolation in the field of educational ideas.

Barnard's original proposal to the American Association for the Advancement of Education, as noted earlier, included a plan for an "American Library of Education." From the beginning of his editorship of the *Journal,* Barnard kept this goal in mind. The library was to be based upon articles from the *Journal* grouped under appropriate subjects. Eventually, large portions of the *Journal* were reprinted as separate volumes. Each article in the *Journal* was started on a new page to facilitate use of the type without incurring the additional expense of new typesetting. Among the works compiled in this fashion were: *Reformatory Education; Papers on Preventive, Correctional and Reformatory Institutions and Agencies in Different Countries* (1857); *Military Schools and Courses of Instruction in the Science and Art of War, Drawn from Recent Official Reports and Documents* (1872); *True Student Life; Letters, Essays and Thoughts on Studies and Conduct; Addressed to Young Persons by Men Eminent in Literature and Affairs* (1873); *Superior Education; an Account of Universities and Other Institutions of Superior Instruction in Different Countries* (1873); *Papers on Froebel's Kindergarten, with Suggestions on Principles and Methods of Child Culture in Different Countries* (1881); *American Educational Biography; Memoirs of Teachers, Educators, and Promoters and Benefactors of Education, Science and Literature* (1874); *American Pedagogy; Contributions to the Science and Art of Teaching by American Educators and Teachers* (1860); *Educational Aphirisms and Suggestions, Ancient and Modern* (1860); *English Pedagogy; Education, the School and the Teacher in English Literature* (1862); *German Pedagogy; Education, the School and the Teacher in German Literature* (1876); *National Education; Systems, Institutions, and Statistics of Public Education in Different Countries* (1872); *Object Teaching, and Oral Lessons on Social Science and Common Things* (1860); *Pestalozzi and Pestalozzianism* (1862); and *Science and Art; Systems, Institutions and Statistics of Scientific Instruction, Applied to National Industries in Different Countries* (1872).

Before the *American Journal of Education* was established, Barnard began his literary career with such works as *School Archi-*

tecture; or Contributions to the Improvement of School-Houses, which went through six editions; *Normal Schools, and Other Institutions, Agencies and Means Designed for the Professional Education of Teachers* (1851); *National Education in Europe; Being an Account of the Organization, Administration, Instruction, and Statistics of Public Schools of Different Grades in the Principal States* (1854); and of course numerous reports associated with his work in Connecticut and Rhode Island, e.g., his *Report on the Condition and Improvement of the Public Schools of Rhode Island* (1846). Altogether, a complete bibliography of substantial works written or edited by Barnard would run to at least seventy-five separate titles, relating to a wide variety of subjects.

Unfortunately, most of Barnard's writings were pitched at too high a level for the readers toward whom they were aimed. The fact was recognized by Barnard. Commenting on the reception of the *American Journal of Education,* he wrote:

The first year's experience convinced me that a very small proportion of those engaged in teaching either high or elementary schools, or in administering State or city systems, or of professed friends of popular education, would labor, spend, or even subscribe for a work of this character; and indeed that the regular subscription list would not meet the expense of printing and paper.[11]

Barnard received both praise and blame for the superior quality and heavy reading nature of the *Journal.* Various suggestions were made to the editor for popularizing the *Journal* in order to increase its paid circulation. Barnard continued, however, to resist the idea of producing a more readable periodical, and therefore the *Journal* always had limited appeal for the large majority of teachers in America's nineteenth-century schools. Barnard's announced ideal and purpose "to embrace only articles of permanent value and interest" ran contrary to the teachers' desire for practical suggestions, such as methods, devices, and classroom aids for everyday use in the schools. Nevertheless, by personal sacrifices, by subscriptions, and by the sale of sets, Barnard carried on until 1878, at which time he wrote to the educator R. H. Quick:

The publication of the *Journal* has proved pecuniarily disastrous. The subscriptions paid in from year to year, have never met the expenses of publication. My small income has been reduced by the deprivation of office and the pressure of the times. No publisher can be induced to undertake the responsibility of the *Journal;* and to carry on the work to a point where the encyclopedic scope of the undertaking could be seen and appreciated has involved my little property in mortgages and myself in obligations which I am now making a desperate effort to meet. If I am successful in disposing of enough sets or volumes of the *Journal* to meet the obligations which mature before the first day of May, I shall continue the publication to the close of Volume XXVIII. If I am not successful, the plates (25,000 pages with more than 1,000 illustrations of school structures) which have cost over $40,000, will go into the melting-pot for type-metal and the volumes on hand will be sold to buyers who may apply within a given time, and at the expiration of that time, will be converted into pulp by the papermakers, and the avails thus realized will be applied, as far as they go, to meet my obligations; and thus will end with me an enterprise which has absorbed my best energies for the last twenty years.[12]

The calamity was averted by prompt action on the part of Quick, William T. Harris, and other American and European educators. In a circular addressed to New England superintendents, Quick wrote, "I would as soon hear that there was talk of pulling down one of the cathedrals and selling the stones for building materials!"[13] Friends rallied to Barnard's support, the crisis was passed, and the *Journal* was continued four years longer. In the editor's old age, a company was formed to take over the plates of the work and thus make Barnard's last years financially more comfortable. After his death, a final volume (Number XXXII), made up of some of Barnard's remaining papers, was published.

Despite the lack of financial success, educational leaders realized their debt and paid tribute to Barnard and his *Journal.* John Stuart Mill, writing in the *Westminster Review,* noted that "England has as yet nothing in the same field worthy of comparison with it."[14] And President Daniel Coit Gilman of Johns Hopkins University commented: "It is the best and only general authority in respect to the progress of education in America in the past century. The comprehensiveness of this work and its persistent publication under adverse circumstances entitle the editor to the grateful recognition of all investigators of our systems of instruction."[15]

CHAPTER 7

Producing Better Teachers

F ROM the outset of his campaign for public school improvement, Henry Barnard recognized that the key factor was better
qualified teachers. Such related considerations as regular attendance, grading, school buildings, finances, and proper legal provisions would be of little avail until teaching personnel could be
strengthened. One device for this purpose, Barnard concluded,
would be to attract better teachers through better salaries.

A prerequisite for obtaining the improvements visualized, however, was to raise teaching in the common school to the level of a
profession, and that demanded specialized training. The day of
"school-keeping," Barnard asserted, had passed. In his first speech
before the Connecticut Legislature, in 1838, when he introduced an
"act to provide for the better supervision of Common Schools,"
Barnard stated "that it is idle to expect good schools until we have
good teachers. With better teachers will come better compensation
and more permanent employment. But the people will be satisfied
with such teachers as they have, until their attention is directed to
the subject, and until we can demonstrate the necessity of employ-
ing better, and how they can be made better by appropriate training
in classes and seminaries, established for that specific purpose."[1]
The following year, in another address, to the Connecticut House
of Representatives, Barnard further expressed his faith in the professional training of teachers: "Give me good teachers, and in five
years I will not work a change, but a revolution in the education of
the children of this State. I will not only improve the results, but the
machinery, the entire details of the system by which these results
are produced."[2]

An unconvinced Legislature refused a proposed appropriation of

61

$5,000 to finance a teachers' institute. Undaunted, the Secretary of the Board proceeded at his own expense. Barnard issued an invitation to teachers of Hartford County to meet for several days in Hartford, where they would be given lessons in the teaching of reading, composition, arithmetic, geography, use of globes, and hear lectures on the theory and practice of teaching by competent instructors, all appointed and paid by Henry Barnard. Twenty-five teachers responded. The stated object was "to show the practicability of making some provision for the better qualification of common school teachers, by giving them an opportunity to revise and extend their knowledge of the studies usually purused in district schools, and of the best methods of school arrangements, instruction and government, under the recitations and lectures of experienced and well-known teachers and educators."[3] Portions of each day were devoted to general discussion and to visiting the best schools of Hartford. Here was perhaps the first regular teachers' institute, a type of training which soon achieved national popularity.

In a biography of Barnard, published in 1855, Noah Porter, later President of Yale University, commented, "Since that Teachers' Class or Institute was held in Hartford in the Autumn of 1839, hundreds of similar gatherings have been held in different states, and thousands and hundreds of thousands of teachers have had their zeal quickened, their professional knowledge increased, their aims elevated, and the schools which they subsequently taught, made better."[4]

The creation of a professional corps of educators was hampered by the lack of any systematic ideas on pedagogy or sound principles of scholarship. Ideological treatises on teaching made frequent references to Pestalozzi, Fellenberg, Rousseau, Lancaster, and the European educational systems as models of various educational practices. In effect, however, the methods of the teachers' institutes have been compared with those of religious evangelicals of the 1830s. Educational literature stressed a teacher's moral character and personal qualities, rather than dealing with the learning process. As aptly described by Paul H. Mattingly, in discussing the teachers' institute, "For the first generation of professional educators this institution made explicit more than any other educational agency how determined schoolmen were to equate professionalization with 'awakening' of moral character rather than with training in uniform measures and standard techniques of teaching."[5] By the 1850s, teachers had begun to alter their views on effective professional preparation and "changed the conception of a teacher from something akin to an evangelical minister into a professional with technical training in pedagogy."[6]

In Barnard's mind, the normal school was the preferred medium for teacher training. His European travels had convinced him of the success and effectiveness of normal schools and he was one of the first American educational leaders to urge their establishment here. When he failed to gain support for such an institution in Connecticut or Rhode Island, Barnard concluded that teachers' institute classes, conducted twice a year for three years, were an adequate substitute for normal school preparation. Shortly after becoming Rhode Island State Superintendent of Education, he succeeded in having legislation passed that required institutes to be held in each county annually.

At the same time, Barnard continued actively to promote the idea of normal schools. The legislature of Rhode Island, in 1844, encouraged him to present a new school statute incorporating such an institution. Barnard brought in a plan proposing two normal schools, one in Providence and one elsewhere in the state. The year following, a bill was passed authorizing the establishment of a normal school, but providing no appropriation to make the law effective. Private financing was suggested in vain. Consequently, nothing happened immediately. Barnard had planted the germ of the idea, however, and in 1854 the Rhode Island general assembly enacted legislation to establish a state normal school at Providence, the forerunner of the Rhode Island Normal School, now Rhode Island College. Two years later, School Commissioner Robert Allyn reported to the general assembly:

The effect of the graduates of the normal school is already felt to some extent for good upon the teachers of the state. They have gone abroad into various schools, and by coming into contact with other teachers, and by making popular the methods of instruction learned in the normal school, they are gradually but surely causing the standard of attainments in schoolteachers to rise, as well as the standard amount of duties they shall be required to perform. If such an influence begins to be apparent within two years from its commencement, we may with certainty expect that its benefits will constantly increase till all parts of our state shall feel it and be made better thereby.[7]

Meanwhile, Henry Barnard had returned to Connecticut, where he assumed the combined position of State Superintendent of Schools and principal of the New Britain Normal School, founded in 1849. During its first year, the New Britain school enrolled 154 students. It survives today under the name of Central Connecticut State College.

Wisconsin was another state destined to be influenced by Barnard's campaign for better prepared teachers. Again, he accepted a double responsibility when, in 1859, he became Chancellor of the University of Wisconsin and agent of the board of normal regents of the state. One of the important matters under discussion in Wisconsin at the time was the question of training of teachers. In 1857 the Legislature had established a new school fund derived from the income of the state's extensive land holdings. Arrangements were made for dividing the income among such high schools, academies, and colleges as would accept examination and supervision by a board of state normal regents. A normal department was also established in the University, along with setting up a chair of pedagogy. Teachers' institutes were being held in a number of counties in the state, and several institutions had drawn upon the funds for normal instruction.

Barnard's duties as agent of the normal board of regents were "to visit and exercise a supervising control over the normal departments of all such institutions as shall apply for a participation in the normal-school fund, to conduct teachers' institutes and normal instruction in the same, and to co-operate with the superintendent of public instruction in procuring a series of public educational addresses to be delivered in various parts of the state."[8] In the fall of 1859 some 20 teachers' institutes were held under Barnard's direction in as many counties in the state. In addition to giving direct instruction to approximately 1,500 teachers at the institutes, he addressed audiences totaling more than 12,000 at his evening lectures.

Barnard was also active with his pen. While in Wisconsin, he was a prolific writer on school organization and methods of teaching; his *Papers for Teachers* were published at his own expense and distributed to the teachers and school officials of the state. He also appeared before the Wisconsin State Teachers Association and outlined his plans for the reorganization of the state's school system. Unfortunately, ill-health forced Barnard's resignation before he had had an opportunity to carry out the ambitious educational reforms he had planned for the common schools and the training of teachers. In his *Public Education in Wisconsin,* Conrad E. Patzer comments, "It is safe to assume that had Barnard been able to apply his organizing abilities for a few years in Wisconsin our state would have secured a unified and modern system of education at that early time."[9]

Massachusetts, under the driving enthusiasm of Horace Mann, was first in the nation in establishing normal schools, starting in 1839 at Lexington. In New York, the first normal school opened its doors in 1844, followed a few years later by similar institutions in Pennsylvania and Ohio. Elsewhere, too, the creation of state normal schools to strengthen public education was stimulated by the labors of Henry Barnard.

Another important contribution to the teaching field was made by Barnard during his stay in Connecticut. To him, a normal school could not perform its mission effectively without a model school attached, where students could practice on live children under expert supervision. "To set up a Teachers' Seminary without a model school," he insisted, "is like setting up a shoemaker's shop without leather."[10] Upon Barnard's urgent recommendation, a state law was enacted to add a model school to the normal school at New Britain.

The acute need for drastic changes in the preparation of teachers in the mid-nineteenth century, when Henry Barnard and Horace Mann were campaigning so vigorously for formal training for the profession, is revealed by an examination of current conditions. School teachers were a transient population, mainly young men under twenty-two and the elderly, constantly on the move. Of nearly 1,300 teachers in Connecticut in 1839, only about one-tenth had taught in the same school before. The only safeguard against incompetence was certification by the district committee, which often acted according to personal bias or with an eye to economy. Men received on the average about sixteen dollars per month and women about half as much. No less demeaning was the prevailing custom of "boarding around," the teacher stretching his or her meager means by living with different families in the community. From such an environment, ambitious teachers escaped as quickly as possible into private schools.

In discussing the recurring problem of teacher turnover, always plaguing the schools, Barnard's first annual report as Secretary to the Board of Commissioners of Common Schools in Connecticut comments:

Nearly one month of the year is practically lost in the time consumed by the teacher in getting acquainted with the temper, wants, dispositions, and previous progress of his various pupils, with a view to their proper classification, and to the adaptation of his own peculiar modes of government and instruction. By the time the school is in good progress, the scholars begin to drop away, the school money is exhausted, and the school dismissed. After a vacation of unnecessary length, as far as the recreation and relief of the children are concerned, the summer school commences with reduced numbers, under a less vigilant supervision, with a poorly compensated teacher, to go through the same course as before; and so on from year to year. The loss of time consequent on the change of teachers, and the long intermission between the two seasons of schooling, not only retards the progress of the school, but leads to the breaking up of regular habits of study, which will be felt in the whole future life.[11]

The future of the teaching profession depended greatly upon proper selection procedures for admission to the normal schools. As expressed in Barnard's fifth Connecticut report, "To determine as far as human judgement *can determine,* the *adaptation* of its pupils for the profession of teaching" was a major function of the normal school. Such innate qualities as "a tact and talent for teaching and governing others" were emphasized. Health was also stressed, represented by "a vigorous and buoyant constitution" and "a fund of lively, lovely, cheerful spirits," for "much of the punishment of our schools comes from a bad digestion in the teacher." Moral and religious purity and strength of character were desirable, along with good manners, "the *manner* as well as the *matter* of the Golden Rule." There should not only be a real desire to teach, but also a love and understanding of children. Important, too, was common sense, "a quality too often wanting in young teachers and only to be acquired by looking at things as they are, and studying to make the most of surrounding circumstances."[12]

Barnard's views on the academic preparation of teachers — a controversial issue down to the present day — were also made clear in his fifth Connecticut report. He rejected "the idea that a person who does not understand a subject thoroughly, can ever teach that subject well." In his opinion, teacher training institutions must stand for scholarship in academic fields as well as professional training. There was no substitute for thorough academic study and none for practical training.

The curriculum of the New Britain Normal School was developed under Barnard's guidance. As described in his fifth Connecticut report, "By means of the regular classes in the Normal School and in the Schools of Practice, an opportunity will be offered to every member of the school to review thoroughly any one or all of the elementary studies required to be taught in the common schools of the state, and to extend his attainments in any of these studies, and such kindred branches as will facilitate his success as a teacher in any grade of common schools."[13] The students were given constant blackboard practice and instruction in the use of maps and cheap and simple apparatus. The program included educational and child psychology, the history of education, "the art of teaching and its methods, and the applications of these methods to each particular study," "the object and principles of public instruction in general and of our system in particular," and general problems of administration, such as "the legal position and relations of the teacher," school architecture, and the "peculiarities of the district school, as well as of other grades of schools.''

English was stressed as of paramount importance, with the aim of giving each child "not only the ability to spell and read with accuracy and facility, but to converse and compose in it with a good degree of readiness and power, and at the same time acquire an earnest and discriminating taste for the choicest productions of American and English literature."[14] Penmanship and drawing were taught, along with some instruction in music and physiology, and some practical training in bookkeeping, agricultural chemistry, and domestic economy.

Henry Barnard was always a strong advocate of woman's education, as previously noted, and his missionary fervor in this field carried over into efforts to increase the number of women teachers in the school system. In his time, women were just emerging from the shelter of their homes to take charge of primary schools in summer. Barnard was able to point proudly to the fact, after a great deal of labor on his part, that "the introduction of a large number of female teachers, in winter as well as in summer, has greatly improved the discipline, moral influence, and *manners* of the Rhode Island public schools."[15] Echoing similar sentiments expressed by Horace Mann in Massachusetts, Barnard wrote in an editorial for the *American Journal of Education,* June 1857:

Our experience in New England has already shown, not only the capacity of women, but their superiority to the male sex, in the whole work of domestic and primary instruction, not only as principal teachers of infant and the lowest class of elementary schools, but as assistants in schools of every grade in which girls are taught, and as principal teachers, with special assistants in certain studies, in country schools generally. Their more gentle and refined manners, purer morals, stronger instinctive love for the society of children, and greater tact in their management, — their talent for conversational teaching, and quickness in apprehending the difficulties which embarrass a young mind, and their power, when properly developed and sustained by an enlightened public sentiment, of governing the most wild and reckless dispositions....[16]

Barnard held no rigid and inflexible views concerning ways and means of producing competent, well-prepared teachers. In his first annual report, he discussed some thirteen different types of institutions or agencies which were capable of providing for the "preliminary training and subsequent professional improvement of teachers." The disadvantage, as he saw it, of a department in a purely academic institution was that it might be regarded as a mere appendage because of "the present comparatively low social and literary position accorded to the teaching profession, in public estimation." The probabilities of producing successful teachers, Barnard was convinced, were greatest in normal schools. He pointed out that, "One acquainted with normal schools, and the advantages to schools of whatever grade of teachers well instructed in the *art of teaching,* must know that a person thoroughly educated at a normal school is likely to be far better prepared to be principal of an academy, or a high school, than a graduate from any college which does not furnish a course of instruction and discipline in this scholastic art."

Nevertheless, Barnard did not insist upon perfectionism where ideal means were impracticable or unattainable. Accordingly, he favored teachers' institutes, libraries, the publication and circulation of books and periodicals, and close supervision of teachers. The essential aim was for teachers to acquire knowledge, together with the art and science of teaching it. How this could best be achieved should be determined "by looking at things as they are, and studying to make the most of surrounding circumstances."[17]

CHAPTER 8

European Influences

A deep interest in European educational methods and systems among American educators in the mid-nineteenth century and earlier led to many visits abroad. Reports, based on firsthand experience, by Alexander D. Bache, professor of physics and president of Girard College in Philadelphia, and Calvin E. Stowe, Ohio educator, were widely read. Even more famous, as well as controversial, were Horace Mann's observations published in his *Seventh Annual Report,* 1843. Victor Cousins, French minister of instruction, had produced a report on education in Prussia, an influential document which was soon translated into English and found many American readers. Americans attending German universities had observed and reported on education in the German states, and Bronson Alcott had introduced Pestalozzian ideas to a group of Massachusetts teachers.

The first of Henry Barnard's five European tours occurred in 1835–36, during which time he spent nearly a year traveling through Great Britain and the Continent. Armed with letters of introduction to every distinguished person he wanted to meet, he set out to interview some of Pestalozzi's disciples and to discuss theories of education with the principal European educators. Traveling mainly on foot, Barnard covered large portions of England, Scotland, and Switzerland. His primary interest was in studying social, municipal, scholastic, charitable, and political conditions. The first letter to his family, written from London, however, was about mundane matters:

In making my preparations for my English tour, I exchanged my hat for one some two or three inches lower in its crown, but which is made up in

70

an extra inch on the heel of my boot. Thus booted, hatted, and coated, you would hardly distinguish my outward man from the Englishmen around me at this hotel, the Adelphi.[1]

Thus in the costume of a conventional Englishman, to avoid being spotted as an awkward countryman from America, Barnard met his idol, Lord Brougham, and discussed with him the best agencies to secure universal education. William Wordsworth was out in the hayfield, dressed in "a brown frock coat, plaid pantaloons, and a broad-brimmed straw hat," when young Henry arrived to call upon him. The two discussed the art of poetry. Other visits were to Thomas Carlyle, Thomas DeQuincey, and John Gibson Lockhart. Across the Channel, Barnard conferred with Emanuel Fellenberg, educator and agriculturist, and other Swiss educators, and stayed for a time in Paris with Edwin Forrest, American actor.

Wherever Barnard went, in England, France, Germany, and Switzerland, he found education considerably more advanced than in America, and he came home to Hartford in 1836 more deeply convinced than ever of the necessity for "basing all our hopes of permanent prosperity on universal education." His great appreciation of Heinrich Pestalozzi and of German education began with these first European travels. Through conversations with some Pestalozzian disciples, Barnard learned more and more about Pestalozzi's philosophy and became fully converted to the belief that these ideas provided the best possible basis for modern elementary education. Originally, Barnard's plans had included an extended stay in Berlin to study civil law, a plan abandoned because of his father's illness.

Barnard did not return to Europe until 1852, after he had established his reputation as a leader of American education. This trip abroad was made primarily for his health, though he also gathered much valuable information. Two years later, the Governor of Connecticut commissioned him as a delegate to the International Exposition of Educational Methods, meeting in London. When he attended the centennial dinner of the Society of Arts in the Crystal Palace, he was accorded special honors. His fame had spread abroad. Later, the acquaintances and friendships gained at the Exposition were valuable to Barnard in editing the *American Journal of Education*. From the outset, contributions from foreign educators were a major feature of the journal.

All departments of the Exposition were visited by Barnard, and there for the first time he saw a kindergarten in operation. A model kindergarten was being taught by Madame Rongé, who was putting into practice the theories long advocated by Barnard for American schools. The spirit of Pestalozzi's ideas prevailed, with dedicated women teachers, a model schoolhouse and schoolroom, and small children visibly developing under the eyes of the teachers. Barnard bought a small statue of Froebel, "father of the kindergarten," for his study at home. Thereafter on many occasions he spoke on Froebel's ideas and the technical practice of the kindergarten from the point of view of an eyewitness.

Unquestionably, the most important product of Barnard's travels abroad, his interest in European education, and his contacts with European educators is found in the files of the *American Journal of Education*. As noted earlier, the journal brought to its readers an amazingly complete record of foreign educational thought and experience — all in the English language, original or in translation. At the same time, while recognizing the value of European educational concepts, Barnard recognized the necessity for adaptation to American institutions and to the American environment.

Even before the founding of the *American Journal of Education*, Barnard had produced a major work entitled *National Education in Europe; Being an Account of the Organization, Administration, Instruction, and Statistics of Public Schools of Different Grades in the Principal Cities* (Hartford, 1854), an 890-page opus arranged by countries, beginning with Germany and the German states, and proceeding through Austria, Switzerland, France, and a dozen other nations, concluding with England.

Like Henry Wadsworth Longfellow, Barnard believed, as previously pointed out, that the distinctive aspects of American culture were basically Western European. Hence his emphasis on the study of comparative education. As a leader in the public school revival,

Barnard found it useful to employ the most recent intellectual currents from across the Atlantic to stimulate American educational thought and to shape American educational institutions. Educational policies formed on narrowly nationalistic lines or that were based on provincial isolationism, he was convinced, lost much of solid value.

Before the *American Journal of Education* was established, Barnard had discovered that much educational literature and educational history were inaccessible in the English language. He therefore announced that "to supply this deficiency is one of the cardinal objects of this Journal."[2] The editor deplored the failure to profit from past experience and from the experience of others. In part, that fact could be attributed to a gap in the backgrounds of most American educators of the time, who, as Barnard noted, had been deprived "of any thing like a scientific training in their profession" and therefore knew little of the history of education. A consequence was that Barnard's fellow Americans were likely "to re-invent modes and ideas which have been tried and given up before, and thus to spend precious months, or years even, in pursuing and detecting errors which a small knowledge of the history of their profession would have prevented them from practicing for a moment, and would have taught them carefully to avoid."[3] The "modern improvements" which these educators wasted their time and talent in rediscovering, Barnard pointed out had been conceived and developed some seventy years before by Pestalozzi or more than two centuries earlier by Comenius.

To Barnard, as to his other historically minded contemporaries, Heinrich Pestalozzi was a heroic leader of the educational advance. The successful adaptation of Pestalozzian philosophy and principles in Germany and especially in Prussia during the early nineteenth century deeply impressed educators in Europe and in America. The first full account of Pestalozzi and his progressive educational ideas to appear in the *Journal,* as noted earlier, was a translation of Von Raumer's biographical study, serialization of which began in the June 1857 issue. Barnard found particularly appealing Pestalozzi's faith in education as a means of regenerating society and his views on ways of humanizing education. Accordingly, the *Journal* published a full account of the famous Swiss educator, his principles as revealed in his major writings, the story of his disciples, the spread and influence of his ideas, and descriptions of Pestalozzian methods and practice, both at Yverdon and in schools in Germany and elsewhere.

The *Journal* also made available in English translation Pestalozzi's own writings. The March 1859 issue carried the *Evening Hours of a Hermit*, a key to Pestalozzi's educational views. Later in the same year, over 200 pages were devoted to Pestalozzi and to long selections from his writings. Most of the original volume of *Leonard and Gertrude* was published from a British translation. Extracts were also reprinted from another celebrated social novel, *How Gertrude Teaches Her Children*. Subsequently, these scattered materials were brought together by Barnard in his *Pestalozzi and His Educational System* (Syracuse, N.Y., 1874). On receiving a copy of the book, Von Raumer wrote the editor from Erlangen: "You have collected with the greatest diligence all that relates to Pestalozzi and his school. . . . It is the most comprehensive, reliable, and satisfactory work I have on the great Swiss educator."[4]

A special aspect of Pestalozzi's teachings was the subject of another Barnard work, *Object Teaching,* published in 1860, which helped to gain enthusiastic acceptance of Pestalozzian principles when they were introduced by Edward A. Sheldon at Oswego. Richard Emmons Thursfield aptly observes:

Pestalozzi's conception of education, his tender consideration of the child, his exaltation of the teacher, his use of sense perception, his emphasis upon the natural and harmonious development of the whole child — the head, the heart, and the hand — and his conviction that the child could be vastly molded by his environment, were appealing ideas for the young republic which had been nurtured in the doctrine of natural rights and the humanitarianism of the Enlightenment.[5]

In searching for a comprehensive history of European education to present to his readers through the columns of the *American Journal of Education,* Barnard, as already noted, settled upon Karl Von Raumer's four-volume *History of Pedagogy.* Installments, in English translation, of this monumental work are scattered through nine volumes of the *Journal.* Von Raumer's treatment of educational history doubtless struck a sympathetic chord in Barnard's nature because of the former's democratic and liberal attitudes, his humanitarian zeal, his Protestant convictions, and his insistence that it was the duty of the state to provide education. Altogether, more than 1,300 pages in the *Journal* were devoted to the translation of Von Raumer's history of European education dating from the early Renaissance down to "our time."

Barnard drew heavily, also, upon other German sources, which he considered "pre-eminently rich" in the history of education as well as in principles and methods of instruction, "from infant training to the broadest university culture." Of the foreign studies dealing with education published in the *Journal,* 43 percent were concerned with German education.

Another large block of material was derived from British sources — some 40 percent of the whole. British books, journals, pamphlets, newspapers, and documents were mined for pertinent literature relating to the history of education and comparative education. British discussions of the function of education, of the value of the classics, and the content of the curriculum were likewise included. The wide variety of British published sources provided Barnard with materials for his compilation of articles on English charity schools, parochial schools, Sunday schools, infant schools, reformatory schools, special schools, teacher-training schools, universities, other educational facilities, and government provision and aid for education.

The historical view of British educational thought was represented in the *Journal* by such works as Sir Thomas Elyot's *The Governour* (1531), Robert Ascham's *Scholemaster* (1570), John Milton's *Tractate on Education* (1644), and John Locke's *Some Thoughts Concerning Education* (1693). Other writings ranged down into the nineteenth century. For example, Herbert Spencer's *Education: Intellectual, Moral and Physical* was reproduced in the *Journal,* in 1862, within a year after publication in book form. Other well-known literary names appearing in the *Journal* were Oliver Goldsmith and Samuel Johnson, but, for reasons unknown, nothing was picked up from Dickens, Thackeray, or Ruskin.

Aside from Germany and Britain, Barnard rounded out the history of education in the Western world by French, Austrian, Russian, Dutch, Belgian, Norwegian, Swedish, Spanish, Greek, and Italian writings. Neither were ancient authors neglected: selections from the works of Plutarch, Quintilian, Plato, and Aristotle were published from time to time.

The field of biography was of special interest to Barnard, and the pages of the *Journal* reflect his concern by presenting biographies of educational leaders of all periods. Some of the sketches were obtained from histories, reference works, and periodicals; others were portrayed in articles specifically prepared for the *Journal*. In the latter category were the lives of two individuals highly admired by the editor: Thomas Arnold and Lord Brougham.

Also solicited by Barnard for the *Journal* were firsthand accounts from American students who had recently studied special types of educational institutions in Europe. One such person was young Daniel Coit Gilman, later president of the University of California and of Johns Hopkins University, who reported some of his observations upon "Scientific Schools in Europe" in the first volume of the *Journal*.

Barnard saw the field of education in broad perspective. Thus he gathered material on all phases of technical instruction. One issue of the *Journal,* in September 1862, as the American Civil War was raging, was devoted to military education in France and Prussia. The liberal definition of the term "education" is demonstrated, too, by articles on the history and current status of agricultural and industrial education, of music and art as branches of education, on naval education, on museums and exhibitions as educational agencies, workingmen's education, lyceums and popular lectures, and on the educational activities of learned societies.

The history of American education could hardly be understood or written without recognizing its European intellectual and educational background. Henry Barnard, through his *American Journal of Education,* played a principal role in making the European experience available to American readers. The concepts of state supervision, compulsory education, and universal education derived from Prussia and the other German states profoundly influenced American educational development. Also transplanted from the same source came American ideas concerning teacher training, grading, and methodology. Higher education in America, modeled on British institutions, experienced great changes from studies of German, French, and English examples. German and French models did much to shape American scientific, agricultural, and industrial education.

Barnard in 1840, in a statement defending Horace Mann, asserted that "An enlightened community would disdain the contracted view that forbids men to look abroad for improvement." Richard E. Thursfield added, "Barnard through his *Journal* demonstrated his own conviction that there should be no isolation in the realm of educational ideas."[6]

CHAPTER 9

Educational Organization

T HE subject of educational organization has various facets: the government of the schools in local communities, teaching methods, the grading of schools, the curriculum, physical facilities, etc. Henry Barnard concerned himself with all aspects.

The contemporary state of affairs, insofar as public schools were involved, when Barnard first began to study educational problems was truly deplorable. In his reports, Barnard uses such descriptions as "the miserable district schools," the "utterly abominable methods," the "harsh and demoralizing discipline," and the "pitiful compensation of teachers." From every point of view, common schools were poorly equipped and inadequately supported. There were no institutions for the professional training of teachers and few school libraries.

Among the steps which Barnard proposed to remedy the situation were these: to raise the status of teaching by making it a well-paid, permanent profession open only to educated individuals; to build comfortable, conveniently located schoolhouses and to equip them properly; to establish libraries for both the schools and the adult population of every town; to improve instruction through a revised curriculum, suitable grading of children, and better teaching methods. Some of these topics, such as normal schools and libraries, have been dealt with elsewhere; others will be considered here.

I School Buildings

Barnard was a pioneer in the planning of school buildings. His *School Architecture; Or, Contributions to the Improvement of School-Houses in the United States* is reputed to be the first book on school architecture published in America. The work went through six editions from 1848 to 1860. In the preface Barnard states:

The subject was forced on the attention of the author in the very outset of his labors in the field of public education. Go where he would, in city or country, he encountered the district School-house standing in disgraceful contrast with every other structure designed for public or domestic use. Its location, construction, furniture and arrangements, seemed intended to hinder, and not promote, to defeat and not perfect, the work which was to be carried on within and without its walls. [1]

The close connection between a good school and a good schoolhouse was stressed by Barnard to parents and school officials. Principles which should be taken into account in the planning process, he maintained, were provisions for children differing in age, sex, size, and studies; "for children whose health and success in study require that they shall be frequently, and every day, in the open air, for exercise and recreation, and at all times supplied with pure air to breathe"; for children who would be occupying the building in cold winter and hot summer days; the adjustment of seats and desks for comfort and height; good lighting in every part of the room, avoiding any excess, glare, or reflection; proper air circulation; and uniform heating in different parts of the room, to avoid both chilling and overheating. The comfort and convenience of the teacher must also be considered, through a sufficiently large desk, placed to facilitate supervision of the schoolroom, space for books and apparatus, and a recitation area equipped with blackboard, stands for hanging maps, and all necessary apparatus. [2]

The scarcity of even minimum equipment in the schools of Barnard's time is revealed by his emphasis on the necessity for providing at least one blackboard for each room and a slate, pencil holder, sponge for each desk. Noted also is the desirability of furnishing a schoolroom clock, pictures for the study of geography and history, an inexpensive collection of minerals and specimens or drawings of plants and animals for the study of the natural sciences, and a "magic lantern" with sets of diagrams to illustrate astronomy, natural history, cities, landscapes, and costumes. An essential constituent of a superior school, also, Barnard declares, is a well-selected library.

The chief criteria for the location of a schoolhouse listed by Barnard are that it should be "dry, quiet, pleasant, and in every respect healthy." Strictly to be avoided are a low, damp, bleak, and unsheltered site, a noisy and dirty thoroughfare, and proximity to "places of idle and dissipated resort." The schoolhouse itself should be constructed of the best materials that can be afforded and planned generously as to space to prevent overcrowding.

Barnard's continued attention to and interest in physical facilities are shown by the fact that he devoted more than a thousand pages of the *American Journal of Education* to school architecture. Accompanying this material were over 800 woodcuts of educational structures, including the plans of many newly erected school buildings. Also scattered through the *Journal* were woodcuts illustrating school apparatus and school furniture. Not all the articles were original; a considerable proportion was reprinted from Barnard's *School Architecture* and from his earlier educational reports.

II *Grading of Schools*

The problem of homogeneous grouping of children in schools occupied Barnard's mind throughout his educational career. Progress in that direction was handicapped by the small one-room, one-teacher school. As population grew and larger school buildings were erected, proper grading became more practicable. Another factor was the growing use of the Pestalozzian method of oral instruction which required homogeneous groupings. The difficulties confronting the teacher in the one-room school are elaborated in Barnard's Rhode Island report for 1845.[3] Therein it is pointed out that the age spread may be from four to sixteen, of children of both sexes; while the multiplicity of studies ranged from teaching the alphabet to advanced grammar school subjects, resulting in an excessive number of classes, with scant time for hearing recitations or attention to individual students. Further complications were caused by the diversity of textbooks and variations among the pupils in educational attainment and intellectual capacity.

"An ordinary session of a large public school, whose chaotic and discordant elements had not been reduced to a system by a proper classification" was rated "a farce" by Barnard. What was required, he insisted, was a grouping of pupils by age and attainments. The latter was regarded as particularly important, though a boy of, say, sixteen, deficient in education, should not be placed in a class of small children; to do so would "mortify and discourage him." In large schools, Barnard advocated specialization among teachers in subjects taught.

Three principal divisions of public schools were proposed by Barnard. The first, primary schools, would be designed for children between the ages of three and eight. For these very young children, the schoolroom should be light, cheerful, and "furnished with appropriate seats, furniture, apparatus and means of visible illustration." An attractive playground was as essential as the schoolroom, since "the hours of play and study, of confinement and recreation, must alternate more frequently than with older pupils." Women teachers were recommended by Barnard for this age group.

Intermediate, or what Barnard called secondary, schools would enroll students from ages eight to twelve, approximately. Assuming that the primary school had done its job properly in teaching the rudiments of various subjects, the secondary school should be expected to give students a more thorough knowledge of reading, arithmetic, penmanship, drawing, geography, history, and the use of language in composition and speech. Either male or female teachers were suitable for this level, in Barnard's opinion, though in large schools both should be employed, "as the influence of both are needed in the training of the moral character and manners."

The high school, the third stage, was a new institution at the beginning of Barnard's career. Historically, the first to be established in the United States was the Boston English High School in 1821. In Connecticut, the first fully organized high school was founded in Hartford, in 1847. The prolonged discussion, legislative acts, and controversy preceding the school's creation are described in detail in Orwin Bradford Griffin's *The Evolution of the Connecticut State School System, with Special Reference to the Emergence of the High School* (N.Y., 1928). Henry Barnard played a key role in the movement to establish the Hartford High School. Several years elapsed before the school was completely functioning.

As Barnard viewed the place of the high school in his three-level scheme, its curriculum should embrace a continuation of intermediate school studies, especially the English language and drawing, together with a knowledge of algebra, geometry, and trigonometry and their applications, "the elements of mechanics and natural philosophy and chemistry, natural history, including natural theology, mental and moral science, political economy, physiology, and the constitution of the United States."[4] Articles in the *American Journal of Education* from time to time described the evolution and rapid growth of secondary schools in the United States from the mid-1850s onward.

Barnard also saw the need for several types of supplementary schools, below the college level, for older students deficient in the elementary studies. One such group, he suggested, would be apprentices, clerks, and other employed young people, for whom evening schools might offer studies directly relevant to their jobs.

The proper gradation of schools was perhaps not practicable, Barnard recognized, in sparsely populated areas. If this were the situation, he recommended that "the school terms should be so arranged that during the warm months the district school shall receive only the young children and in the winter months, only the older scholars."[5]

III *Curriculum*

By the beginning of the Barnard era, the curriculum of the common school had come to be solidly based on the three Rs. Under commercial and frontier pressures, such utilitarian subjects as bookkeeping, navigation, and surveying were coming into the high schools, but on the lower levels, at least, there was little variation from the basic subjects. A survey by Barnard, while Secretary to the Board of Commissioners of Common Schools in Connecticut, revealed that spelling, reading, arithmetic, and writing were taught in all the winter schools. In a few of the larger schools, advanced pupils were studying natural philosophy, bookkeeping, chemistry, algebra, and composition, and there were occasional courses in geometry, trigonometry, rhetoric, mental and moral philosophy, and Latin.

Barnard reports that some school districts objected to the teaching of any subjects except spelling, reading, writing, and arithmetic. He himself was averse to undue proliferation of courses, on grounds that they divided the teacher's time and attention, prevented proper classification of pupils, led to a smattering acquaintance with too many branches, and often resulted in the neglect of basic education. In any case, Barnard concluded, the primary goal of the common schools should be "the harmonious development of the whole nature of the child — the physical, intellectual, and the moral powers."[6]

IV *Methods of Instruction*

From early colonial days until well into the nineteenth century, methods of instruction in American schools were static. There had been no critical examination of traditional modes or attempts at innovation. Through knowledge he had gained by wide reading and through his European travels, Barnard was one of the outstanding leaders in spreading new concepts. Some ways to improve instruction, in Barnard's view, were "by reducing the variety of studies, and books; multiplying the number in each class, and adopting those methods of instruction which enable him to act with most effect on a large number and to enlist the interest, and cooperation of the scholars themselves."

Several methods of instruction which he had observed being practiced in the best schools were reviewed by Barnard: (1) *Individual instruction,* calling up the students one by one and adapting the teaching to each personally, was rated "an immense waste of the labor of the teachers." (2) *Simultaneous instruction,* or the practice of addressing questions and explanations to an entire class, to which individuals or the whole class might be expected to respond, a method which Barnard found "keeps every mind attentive" and was well adapted to lessons in spelling, mental arithmetic, geography, and history. (3) *Interrogative or explanatory instruction,* or the practice of questioning the pupil about what he is reading and reciting and then adding any explanations needed to clear up "false notions." (4) *Oral instruction,* a method Barnard found little used in the schools he visited, but which, "in the hands of a teacher properly trained and qualified, gives not only variety and interest to the ordinary exercises of the school, but arouses the mind to general activity." (5) *Exercises on the slate and blackboard* for all studies, a method Barnard believed effective for the instruction of older students and for providing "amusing and useful employment for younger children." (6) *Mutual instruction,* an idea developed by Heinrich Pestalozzi at his school in Stans in the 1790s, when there was an acute shortage of teachers. The essence of the scheme is to use older pupils, properly trained, to teach the younger ones and to assist the teacher in other ways. Barnard reported on a number of experiments with mutual instruction, in Europe and America, with varying success; on the whole, he concluded that under careful and expert guidance the method could be beneficial to the students and to the school.[7]

Barnard held firm views on the teaching of specific subjects. Spelling, he believed, "should be taught in connection with reading and writing, otherwise it becomes of little practical use." Reading should be made "the most attractive, spirited, and useful" subject in school, instead of being "the most toilsome and defective exercise," as it is generally conducted. The teaching of arithmetic should begin with an understanding of first principles and continue with the aim of giving each student a "mastery of the practical application and combination of these principles"; Barnard believed some stress should be placed on teaching "the arithmetic of daily life." Writing, he suggested, should be taught in connection with drawing and composition, with the aim of training the student to put his "thoughts into the form of a business or friendly letter rapidly, legibly, and grammatically." Altogether, Barnard asserted, "The mastery of the English language, combining spelling, reading, grammar and composition, should be the leading object of the district school, as far as intellectual education is concerned."[8]

Barnard was critical of the schools for their neglect of what he considered two important areas. The first was religious and moral instruction, including the failure to make full use of the Bible. "As to physical education," Barnard noted, "there is nothing taught respecting it, except by a practical violation of all its great principles in the location, light, temperature, ventilation, seats and desks, of the school-house."

Barnard was a disciple of Pestalozzi in his advocacy of object teaching. To provide American teachers with a complete exposition of Pestalozzi's views, he published a volume on *Object Teaching* in 1860 and reprinted its contents in the *American Journal of Education*. Additional contributions on the subject, by Barnard and others, continued to appear in the *Journal*. According to Pestalozzi, a child perceives and learns by way of objects — geometrical models, field trips, rock and mineral collections, a hot stove, etc., thus a child given object training will be prepared for a scientific education. The essential principle was to proceed from the near to the remote — building first upon the child's observation of things touched and seen around him in his immediate neighborhood and going from there "in ever widening circles" to more distant objects. Barnard was a thorough convert to this theory, asserting that "the use of some simple apparatus, so as to employ the eye, more than the ear, in the acquisition of knowledge" would "increase ten-fold the efficiency of our common schools." In teaching geography, especially the natural features of the earth, and astronomy, for example, he believed that the use of a globe and a planetarium would reduce the period of learning from months to hours.

The methodology of teaching different subjects was treated by special articles and incidental references in various issues of the *American Journal of Education*. Reading received more than usual attention. A leading article by W. F. Richards, for example, discussed the principal methods — the alphabetic, phonic, phonetic, and the Jacotot system. The last, developed by an early nineteenth-century French writer, Jean Joseph Jacotot, has a modern ring: a pupil should be "at once instructed in reading words at sight, without reference to the letters of which they are composed."[9]

Another feature of the *Journal* was to present courses of study used in different schools, including much detail as to methods, errors to be avoided in teaching, topics to be covered within individual subjects, textbooks to be used with exact page assignments in some cases, and the time to be devoted to music, drawing, and physical exercise.

V *Educational Administration*

With his background of varied experience as an educational administrator, Barnard was always keenly interested in problems of school organization, supervision, and related matters. His perspective was all-inclusive, from the national to state and local levels. In local communities, the tendency had been to divide and subdivide the schools, bringing education as close as possible to the children. The trend was encouraged by poor means of transportation and communication.

The district system of organization of the schools in the state of Connecticut resulted in an average of fifty-two persons in each district. Actually, there were 2,510 districts with less than fifty persons each, causing, Barnard reported, "an alarming inequality in the ability of the districts to maintain good schools."[10] He found "some of the best schools in the state" in the "intermediate districts," numbering between forty and seventy persons, but concluded that they could be further strengthened and improved by more tax revenue, employment of additional teachers, and extension of terms — all of which could be accomplished by mergers of closely adjoining districts. In some cases, the smaller districts existed from necessity, covering a large extent of territory on the outskirts of the school societies. A majority, however, had grown up in order to bring the schoolhouse nearer and nearer to smaller groups of families to accommodate younger children. One consequence was cheap teachers, short terms, and small, crowded school buildings. Thus, Barnard declared, bringing about "a vast inequality in the education of children in different districts."

There were several possible remedies for the situation, according to Barnard: leave the small children in the neighborhood schools and transfer older pupils to larger schools; provide more state financial support for poor schools in outer districts; and increase the minimum number of inhabitants required for creation of a district. Also needed, he stated, was general supervision of the schools in such matters as schoolhouses, examination and employment of teachers, the regulation of studies and textbooks, and classification of students. "The present distribution of powers and duties respecting the presentation, examination and employment, supervision, dismission and payment of teachers," Barnard wrote, "leads to a complexity, and not infrequently conflict of jurisdiction, that defeats the great objects of the law, which, as I understand, are to bring good teachers, and only good teachers, into the schools."[11]

VI *Attendance*

The regularity of school attendance was a major problem in Connecticut and Rhode Island, Barnard found, as Horace Mann was discovering in neighboring Massachusetts. He revealed himself to be a devoted follower of Pestalozzi in believing that the family circle and the mother were the best school for young children, under ideal conditions, but the environment in densely populated sections of cities and in all manufacturing villages was so shockingly bad, "it is better for children to be removed as early and as long as possible from such scenes and such examples, and placed in an infant or primary school, under the care and instruction of a kind, affectionate and skillful female teacher."[12]

Barnard cited some of the evils of non- or irregular attendance. Many students, he noted, were present in the schools for so few months in the year or attended for so short a period of their lives, "that their school education must necessarily be very limited, superficial and incomplete."[13] Elsewhere he adds:

Many scholars in public schools attended so irregularly from day to day, and with such want of punctuality at the opening of each term, and of each half day's session, and withdrew prematurely before the close of the term, or of the daily session, that they derived but little benefit from the schools, and greatly impaired their usefulness, and lowered the scholarship of the public schools.[14]

A large proportion of children over twelve years of age, male and female, were employed in mills, in workshops, or on farms, accounting for much absenteeism. "The cheaper labor of children and females," Barnard charged, was being substituted "for the more expensive labor of able bodied men." Some suggestions for amelioration, if not cure, of the attendance problem, offered by Barnard, were year-round operation of the schools, making it possible for students to attend winter or summer; barring students who arrived after the beginning of a school day; dropping from the rolls students who were absent more than a specified number of days, except for illness or family emergencies; keeping a detailed register or record of attendance; maintaining class records showing each student's attainments and progress; forwarding a weekly or monthly report to parents summarizing individual attendance, recitations, and perhaps behavior; and enacting child labor laws to be strictly enforced. Reservations were held by Barnard about compulsory attendance; he preferred to proceed by securing the cooperation of parents and arousing an enlightened public opinion.

VII *School Supervision*

Several groups, in Barnard's time, were charged with supervision of local schools: (1) a board of school visitors or overseers, responsible for the examination and selection of teachers; under the law "to visit the school twice during each season of schooling, and to exact such exercises as may test the proficiency of the school" (the discharge of which duty, according to Barnard, was "in many places, inefficient, irregular, and formal at best"); and the submission of regular reports on the condition of schools under their supervision; (2) a district committee, a branch of the board of overseers, the chief duty of which was to look after the school's financial interests; and (3) the Board of Commissioners of Common Schools, a statewide agency created at the time that Barnard was appointed its secretary. In Barnard's judgment, if all the governing bodies functioned properly, and in accordance with their mandates, the public schools would be enormously benefited and improved.[15]

CHAPTER 10

Financing Education

A matter of constant concern and controversy in Henry Barnard's time — and in all subsequent periods — was methods of financing the public schools. Early in the nineteenth century, the states which had been granted large blocks of Western land — the so-called "Western Reserve" — frequently used proceeds from the sale of those lands for the support of education. In the beginning, the funds so derived appeared adequate, with little need for local taxation to supplement the federal endowment. As the population grew, however, it became obvious that additional financing was urgently required.

The seriousness of current conditions was revealed in Barnard's reports. Barnard was especially concerned with what he described as the "pitiful compensation of teachers." In his first *Annual Report* (1840), Barnard found that the salary of male teachers in Connecticut, exclusive of board, averaged $15.48 per month; of female teachers, $8.33 per month. He criticized the practice of "boarding around" as harmful to the dignity of teachers. The custom was most embarrassing for the woman teacher, who, in order to secure the privacy she desired, paid for her accommodations out of the pittance called her salary. "Teachers with any degree of self-respect," Barnard asserted, "will not long subject themselves to the annoyance of this mode of begging their bread."[1]

The problem was to convince legislators and the populace at large of the pressing need. The schools had lost the influence of the wealthy and cultivated classes, whose children were attending private schools and who vigorously opposed the added burden of taxation to educate less fortunate children. The masses were equally hostile to school taxes, having become accustomed to depend on state educational funds and being fully persuaded that those expenditures were ample.

Connecticut was a striking example of this state of affairs. As A. D. Mayo comments in his biography of Barnard, "Gradually, more and more, the common school of Connecticut was left as a sort of educational 'house of refuge' for the poorer class; and, as a school for the poor in our country generally becomes a poor school, the decline went on apace."[2] Henry Barnard's dismissal as secretary of the Connecticut Board of Commissioners of Public Schools and the abolition of the Board were attributable in large measure to Barnard's proposal that each school society should raise each year by taxation a sum equal to half that which it received from the state school fund. At the time of Barnard's original appointment, less than 10 percent of the Connecticut school districts imposed taxes for the support of education beyond the meager amounts provided by the state.

Rhode Island's situation, without any public lands, internal or external, to sell, was even more perilous. Whatever was appropriated for public education had to be raised by direct taxation. A further handicap for Barnard, requiring utmost tact and patience, was that he was a "damned Connecticut man" and therefore open to suspicion among Rhode Island's farmers, who took a dim view of educational innovation and "foreigners." Jenkins notes that "the people themselves were indifferent, not only to the need, but to the advantage of good public schools. They were even more prejudiced, on the whole, than the people of Connecticut."[3] To these unenlightened citizens, Barnard's proposal for tax-supported schools approached high treason; at best, it was highhanded robbery. Barnard's notable success in reversing public opinion concerning taxation for schools in both Connecticut and Rhode Island has been described elsewhere.

Early in his career, Barnard eloquently stated his view of the responsibility of the state for education:

In my opinion, it is both just and expedient to provide liberally, but not exclusively, by state endowment, for the support of public instruction. As education is a want not felt by those who need it most, for themselves or their children, it is a duty which avarice and short sighted self-interest may disregard, as it is a right which is inherent in every child, but which the child cannot enforce, and as it is an interest both public and individual which cannot be neglected, it is unwise and unjust to leave it to the sense of parental duty or the unequal and insufficient resources which individuals and local authorities, under the stimulus of ordinary motives, will provide. If it is thus left, there will be the educated few, and the uneducated many. This is the uniform testimony of all history.[4]

To supplement other revenue during Barnard's regime, many districts in Connecticut, Rhode Island, and elsewhere had revived the discriminating colonial rate-bills. Rate-bill was a term applied to bills for tuition when the poor were exempted from paying such bills. A free school was one in which neither tuition nor rate-bills were charged. The schools of Barnard's day frequently used both tuition and rate-bills. The first comprehensive rate-bill statute enacted by Connecticut is dated 1839, while Barnard was secretary of the Board of Commissioners of Common Schools. When the rate-bill law was proposed, Barnard wrote:

It is difficult to frame a law to operate more unfavorably, unequally, and in many cases, more oppressive than this.... There is not only the ordinary pecuniary interest against it, but it is increased from the fact that all the abatements for poor children must come upon them that do attend school.... Again, many of them are just able to pay their own, and the addition of a single penny beyond that is oppressive, so long as its burden is not shared by the whole community.... Again, it is an inducement to parents to keep the children at home, on any trifling demand for their services — for in so doing there is no pecuniary loss sustained; as on the other hand their school bill is by so much diminished.[5]

The rate-bill method, Barnard pointed out further, would become more oppressive as private schools increased and a larger number of the wealthier members of society withdrew their children from the public schools. The burden would therefore be thrown entirely upon the class of people, especially the poor, who sent their children to the common schools. For this reason, Barnard found the school law "radically defective." In fact, he asserted, "The present mode of supporting common schools, principally by public funds and by taxation upon the scholar [pupil] has operated to encourage men of property to abandon them and patronize private schools."[6]

In the same year, Barnard advocated abolition of rate-bills. Instead, he would have property, whether the owners had school-age children or not, as the basis for school support. "This is the cardinal idea," he commented, "of the free school system."[7] Later, in 1845–47, the city of Hartford conducted a campaign to improve its schools and brought Barnard back into the state to assist in the movement. Here, too, he advocated free schools. It was upon his recommendation that the city voted to establish a free high school in 1847. Thus the evidence is clear that up to 1847 Barnard was a champion of free schools.

But when Barnard returned to Connecticut in 1850 as State Superintendent of Schools there were signs of a changing attitude. In the report for his first year, he stated that "a public school is not necessarily a free school. It may be supported by a fund, by a public tax, or an assessment or rate of tuition per scholar, or by any combination of these modes." Local communities should establish such schools on these bases, Barnard argued.[8]

A year later, Barnard had evidently undergone a radical change of opinion, when he recommended that, "Districts and societies should be authorized to establish a rate-bill, or tuition, to be paid by parents or guardians of children at school, graduated according to the class of school, and in no way oppressive to the poor, and diminishing to each family according to the number of children attending school the same term."[9]

In that statement, Barnard adhered to his earlier stand that rate-bills or tuition charges should not be permitted to oppress the poor. The point is reinforced two years later in the wording of a new school law proposed by Barnard: "Every school district, or district committee, when authorized by the district, may establish a rate-bill, or tuition, to be paid by the parents or guardians of the children attending school, provided that no child shall be excluded from any common school in consequence of the inability of his parents or guardians to pay any school tax or rate."[10]

As state advisor of school systems, Barnard urged the people of

Thompsonville, Connecticut, in 1853, to use rate-bills to obtain sufficient income to maintain their schools.

On the other hand, Barnard was one of the signers of a memorial sent in 1855 by the Connecticut State Teachers Association to the legislature urging a change in the state school law, i.e., "To amend the law relating to the mode of supporting schools so as to abolish rate or quarter bills altogether, or to provide that the amount shall be determined before the opening of school, and to be collected in advance."[11]

Except for the 1855 memorial and support for exemption of the poor, it is obvious that after about 1850 Barnard was an advocate of rate-bills as a means of financing the public schools. The switch was important because of his great influence in educational matters. What were the reasons for his reversal of attitude? Barnard himself offered an explanation at a meeting of the American Institute of Instruction, held at Springfield, Massachusetts, in 1856, when he stated:

I am aware that I am uttering a heresy here, but I do not believe that the entire expense of the public schools should rest upon the entire community. I will go as far as the farthest to advocate the most liberal expense to support public schools; but I would always recognize that the duty of educating the child rests primarily with the parent, and that all modes of regulating the expense of the school should be such as to recognize that duty on the part of the parent. I go upon the idea which was original in Massachusetts and Connecticut that half the expense should rest upon the public, and half upon the parent.... I know that the experiment of universal education can succeed where a portion of the expense rests upon the parent. The best education in Europe will be found to exist where the parents contribute to the support of schools. I believe that it is a great mistake, in order to make education universal you must make the schools free.[12]

Barnard's belief was that if every parent was obliged to pay in advance a small sum for his child's tuition, it would correct the problem of non-attendance at school, "because those parents who had paid would feel that in the absence of their children they would lose something they had paid in." Barnard conceded that there were reasons for making the schools free, but maintained that the "necessity of looking after the education of the children is one means of keeping the interest of the parent alive."[13]

Thus the documented facts demonstrate that Barnard was an advocate of free schools until about 1847; by 1850 his views began to change, as is shown by his endorsement of the idea of high schools partially supported by rate-bills or tuition; and by 1851 he came out without reservations for the use of rate-bills as a means of school support.

At the time Barnard was expressing his sentiments, in the early 1850s, the public school forces in Connecticut were attempting to persuade the legislature to abolish rate-bills. The effort was unsuccessful, and doubtless one reason for its defeat was lack of support from Barnard. Not until 1870 was a system of free public schools established in Connecticut.

CHAPTER 11

Books and Libraries

H ENRY Barnard's lifelong passion for books and libraries was
first aroused during his years at the Monson school. He began
at the early age of twelve to buy books and more books. There was
no selfish motive involved in his wide program of reading. His
intention was to inform and to teach others. "Ever since I was conscious of any purpose," stated Barnard, "the aim of my life has
been to gather and disseminate knowledge, useful knowledge —
knowledge not always by the many, but useful to all, to gather it
from sources not always available even to students and scatter it
abroad."[1]

Before entering Yale, Barnard studied advanced Greek and surveying under an able tutor, Abel Flint, and spent a profitable year
in the Hopkins Grammar School. By the time he came to Yale, at
the age of fifteen, he was in the habit of reading extensively in original Greek and Latin literature, chiefly to familiarize himself with
ancient civilizations rather than to learn the languages. A classmate, Noah Porter, wrote that "few professed scholars among us
were as thoroughly familiar with the ancient and modern English
literature as Barnard."[2]

But Barnard was disappointed and irked to discover that he did
not have free access to books in the Yale library. The college library
was not open to underclassmen, though the various society libraries
were available at certain hours to their own members. Barnard
promptly joined Linonia, the debating society, in large part to
enjoy the privileges of its library. In order to have a key and access
to the library when it was closed, he became the assistant librarian,
without salary.

Toward the end of his life, Barnard remarked that he left college "heavily indebted" to one division of the University: the library. As he described the debt:

The College Library was not accessible to students until they reached their junior year.... The whole library, even by the senior students and graduates, was very little used, not much even by the professors. But the libraries connected with the literary societies were accessible, and to that, and the library of the Linonian Society, of which I was a member from the start, I feel under immense obligations. To the privileges of the debates of the society, and the free use of its books, while acting as assistant librarian, in my junior year, and principal librarian in my senior year, I feel myself more largely indebted than to any other agency in that institution.[3]

Eight years after Barnard's graduation from Yale he took the lead in organizing the Hartford Young Men's Institute and became its first president. A primary purpose was to provide a library for the use of the Institute's more than 400 members. A reading room was opened and a collection of 5,000 volumes assembled. Other activities included a series of public lectures and debating groups.

Connecticut had a long tradition of society and parish libraries, preceding Barnard. An article on "Public Libraries in Connecticut," in the *American Journal of Education,* traces the history of such institutions from the early eighteenth century. Barnard quotes with approval a statement by Noah Webster, written in 1789, commending the favorable influence of parish libraries. "They are procured by subscription," Webster explains, "but they are numerous, and have made the desire of reading universal. One hundred volumes of books selected from the best writers, read by the principal inhabitants of a town or village, on ethics, history, and divinity will have an amazing influence in spreading knowledge, correcting the morals, and softening the manners of a nation."[4] Barnard observed that in visiting various parts of the state, between 1838 and 1842, he had seen more than fifty such parish libraries created prior to 1800. He found that these communities had produced a disproportionately large number of college graduates and of persons who had become influential in the professions and public life, compared to parishes and towns where libraries had not been established. "Wherever libraries existed," Barnard added, "it was found that newspapers were more largely taken and read, and a much livelier and more intelligent public spirit prevailed."[5]

In his first report as secretary of the Board of Commissioners of Common Schools, Barnard cited the woeful lack of school libraries in Connecticut. In the entire state in 1839, only six school libraries existed, all except two contributed by public spirited citizens. With almost missionary fervor, Barnard pointed out the numerous "blessings and advantages" which would result from "the establishment of well-selected libraries, adapted not only to the older children in school, but to adults of both sexes, and embracing works on agriculture, manufactures, and the various employments of life."[6]

Perhaps in an effort to shame his fellow citizens and to make them conscious of the state's backward condition in the provision of school libraries, Barnard compared New York's achievements. The state of New York, he reported, had purchased libraries for all of her ten thousand school districts. At the end of 1843, $580,000 was expended by New York for the acquisition of more than two million volumes, and these were accessible to every family and every individual. Barnard considered the contrast with Connecticut's niggardly provision of books "humiliating," especially in view of the state's "more compact and homogeneous" population and its relatively large public funds available for education.

In 1839, Barnard attempted to procure a state appropriation for school libraries. When the effort was unsuccessful, he himself offered to donate a certain number of books for a library in any district which built a schoolhouse of which he approved — thus killing two birds with one stone. The offer was eagerly accepted in a number of towns, and Barnard had the satisfaction of founding the earliest common school library in Connecticut.

Libraries were the most effective instruments for self-education, in Barnard's view. He himself had learned more from books than from teachers and he wished to have others share his experience and good fortune. He commended the New York publishing firm of Harper for assembling a set of books chosen especially for common schools, a collection which cost but twenty dollars, including a bookcase with lock and key.

On another occasion, Barnard wrote, "There are whole neighborhoods in which, with the exception of the Bible, not a single book of any interest or value is to be found. Now of what avail is it to teach a child to read, unless you at the same time furnish him with books?"[7]

Though his success in persuading Connecticut to buy more books was only moderately successful, during his term as secretary, Barnard left two thousand more volumes in libraries of the state in 1842 than there were in 1840. A similar campaign in Rhode Island was more effective. There Barnard obtained at least five hundred volumes for each of twenty-nine school libraries, out of a total of thirty-two towns.

Public libraries open to all, children and adults, were as zealously advocated by Barnard as separate libraries for the schools. His credo is eloquently expressed in a statement appearing in the *American Journal of Education,* in 1865:

Libraries of good books, selected in reference to the intellectual wants of the old and the young, should be provided in every village. To create a taste for reading should be a leading object in the labors of teachers and lecturers. All that the school, even the best, where so much is to be done in the way of disciplining the faculties, all that the ablest lecture, when accompanied by illustrations and experiments, can do toward unfolding the many branches of knowledge and filling the mind with various information, is but little compared with the thoughtful perusal of good books, from evening to evening, extending through a series of years. These are the great instruments of self culture.[8]

Barnard looked beyond the borders of Connecticut to examine the condition of libraries in the United States as a whole in relation to those of Europe. In the first volume of the *American Journal of Education,* he published a statistical table on "Public Libraries in the Principal States, Capitals, and Universities of Europe."[9] Country by country, he tabulated the total number of libraries, the number of volumes of printed books, and the number of manuscripts, followed by a list of the Continent's principal libraries, with the number of volumes held by each, and finally a listing of university libraries with their volume holdings. Barnard's purpose in presenting the data, he wrote, was "to arrest the attention of legislators and men of wealth to the amazing deficiencies of our cities and colleges in the facilities for the profound investigation of any subject of human learning which a great library affords."[10]

A difficult aspect of the book problem in Connecticut, as Horace Mann had found in Massachusetts, was the lack of standardization or uniformity in textbooks. In the first place, the quality was low and there were serious omissions in subjects covered. For example, in his first report as secretary to the Board of Commissioners of Common Schools in Connecticut, after examining a number of texts in general use, Barnard noted, "There is not a single work which gives a sufficiently intelligent account of the principles of our free institutions, of the duties of public officers, and of the relation which every citizen sustains to the state."[11] Also entirely lacking was any work relating to physical education. "The first principles of physiology properly taught, and familiarly illustrated, would be of immense service to society," declared Barnard.

Even more troublesome was the multiplicity of texts used in the schools. No school law existed to regulate the selection of textbooks. The school visitors presumably had the authority to choose the works adopted, but Barnard reported that "I know not of a school society where any very decisive steps have been taken."[12] He went on to point out, "not only is there a great variety in the different schools of the same society, but not infrequently a specimen at least of all these varieties is found in each school."

A preliminary investigation by Barnard revealed that more than two hundred different schoolbooks were being used in the several subjects taught: twelve in spelling, sixty in reading, thirty-four in arithmetic, twenty-one in geography, fourteen in history, nineteen in grammar, four in natural philosophy (science), and forty in other branches.

A prime cause of the diversity of textbooks was the rapid turnover of teachers, a great majority of whom did not remain in the same school for more than a single year. Each teacher had his favorite texts and introduced them wherever he went. Barnard concluded that "the money now expended in the purchase of new books, caused by the change of teachers, would go far to continue the same teacher another month in the same school."[13]

Barnard thought that it was neither desirable nor practicable to obtain uniformity of schoolbooks throughout all of the schools. "The best books it is hoped," he remarked, "have not yet been written in some branches."[14] Nevertheless, he felt that there should be some order and system in the selection procedure. The introduction of a new book in a school depended far more on publishers' enterprise than on parents, teachers, and school officials. Barnard recommended that in future no book would be adopted for school use without approval of a proper committee.

Another problem relating to textbooks was the inadequate supply. Barnard found that teachers were forced in self-defense to purchase books for children whose parents were unable or unwilling to do so; otherwise, there were serious difficulties with student discipline. His solution was to have the district committees furnish the books needed and then add the expense to the school tax of the parent, or in case of inability to pay, the expense should be borne by the whole district or school society. Barnard added a bit of social equality, to make support of education everyone's responsibility: "And it is gross injustice to require of those parents who are just able to pay their own school bills, and furnish their own children with books, to bear the whole expense of the school tax and school bill of those who are unable to pay, while the wealthy, by withdrawing their children altogether from the public schools, escape their share of expense."[15]

The Bible, in Barnard's opinion, could be utilized effectively in the schools for teaching purposes. In schools visited by him he discovered the "Book of Books" being used by teachers in a variety of ways. Some based lessons on ancient geography, history, manners and customs, and moral and religious principles on the Bible. Others considered it a kind of law book to guide human behavior, or viewed it as a literary treasure, or regarded it as offering the best exercises for practice in reading.

Aside from books, Barnard was ahead of his time in promoting the use of "visual aids" in the schools, though Heinrich Pestalozzi had developed visual education and object teaching to a high level in Switzerland some years earlier. Equipment, such as maps and globes or apparatus of any kind, was rare in the Connecticut schools when Barnard came on the scene. There were reported to be only two globes in all the public schools of the state. A feature of the teacher-training programs initiated by Barnard was instruction in the proper use of maps, globes, blackboards, and similar devices.

A love of literature, both classical and modern, is apparent in Barnard's letters and such lectures of his as have survived. Books and the possession of books were a passion with him, and he spared no expense in assembling his own distinguished library. At the time of his death, he owned a personal library of 10,000 volumes of educational literature. Through a gift by J. P. Morgan, the collection is preserved in the Wadsworth Athenaeum on the Trinity College campus, in Hartford, a permanent monument to its creator.

CHAPTER 12

Social and Educational Philosophy

I T is an enlightening exercise to compare the social and educational philosophies of Henry Barnard and Horace Mann. In 1843, Barnard wrote to Mann, "You are my guide, my hope, my friend, my fellow-laborer and fellow-sufferer in 'the cause.'"[1] The views of the two great educational leaders were in harmony in numerous respects. Both concerned themselves with various humanitarian movements. While a member of the Connecticut Legislature, Barnard introduced legislation to improve the condition of the blind and the deaf, the insane, the inmates of jails and prisons, and degraded paupers. He was a supporter of the lyceum movement and friendly toward peace organizations, asserting that the "weight of universal popular intelligence" was on the side of the settlement of international differences without resort to war. Both Barnard and Mann were warm advocates of "liberty of thought, speech, occupation, and political action,"[2] the education of women, and civil service reform.

The most penetrating and perceptive analysis of Barnard's general philosophy comes from the historian Merle Curti in his *Social Ideas of American Educators.*[3] Curti reaches the conclusion that Barnard was more conservative than Mann in a variety of ways, and his conservatism increased with the passage of time — except in education. An example is Barnard's friendliness toward military institutions, revealed in the *Papers on Military Education* published while he was U.S. Commissioner of Education. In the *American Journal of Education* for March 1862, Barnard wrote a eulogistic memorial account of "The Home, the Arm, and the Armory of Samuel Colt," arms manufacturer, praising Colt for providing honest employment to working men, and comparing his ideal of a matchless firearm to that inspiring the noble genius of the sculptor.[4]

Barnard was an early promoter of education for blacks and apparently lacked any serious race prejudice, but he took a much more cautious and discreet position on the slavery issue than did Mann. While Mann, as a member of Congress, was vehemently denouncing the institution of slavery, Barnard maintained friendly relations with Southern leaders, was royally entertained in South Carolina, and was being offered the superintendency of schools in Charleston and New Orleans.

In another important area, Barnard's religious beliefs differed markedly from Mann's. Mann was a Unitarian with broad humanitarian concerns, while Barnard was an Episcopalian, married to a Catholic, and holding to a conservative religious creed. Thus the latter regarded as antireligious, and in the same category, all freethinkers, atheists, deists, and rationalists. Indeed, for Barnard religion and education were inseparable. Christ was the first great teacher. Barnard envisioned a priesthood of teachers, whose training would emphasize reverence for God rather than the intellect. Sunday school teaching was recommended as excellent preparation for public school teaching. The Bible, in Barnard's view, was a basic classroom text for teaching reading, history, geography, and ethical behavior. Curti comments, "When his fundamentalist conception of rationalism and deism is recalled, it is clear that Barnard's attitude tended definitely toward continuing the influence of the colonial religious inheritance."[5]

It is true that Barnard accepted some of the educational doctrines of Rousseau and Pestalozzi, but he rejected Rousseau's general social philosophy as presented in *The Social Contract*. Only the educated man was respected by Barnard; he had little confidence in the general populace, and what he conceived of as its moblike character. His conservative religious indoctrination doubtless influenced Barnard to take a reactionary position on slavery and other forms of social injustice and to refrain from stirring up controversy on controversial issues.

A logical explanation for Barnard's rather rigid social views was that he was born into a well-to-do family and, unlike Mann, did not have to struggle with poverty to obtain an education or to start his career. He was educated at a private school and at Yale, had funds to purchase books, and was able to travel widely at home and abroad, where he met many distinguished men. Among his friends were some of the wealthiest men in America, and Barnard's own investments included sawmills, water works, New York real estate, and Western lands. It should be expected, therefore, that Barnard would have absorbed the characteristic attitudes of men of means.

Holding conservative economic opinions, Barnard denounced Jacksonian democracy for its attacks on the judiciary, on sound money, the national bank, and the protective tariff. He saw the tariff as a bulwark "upon the strength of which a vast amount of property has been invested in manufacturing industry."[6] The courts were guardians of property against the "frenzy of popular excitement," he stated in a speech to the Connecticut House of Representatives.[7]

Barnard's distrust of the hordes crowded into city slums and, in fact, the uneducated laboring class as a whole is reflected in speeches and published writings. From such a source, he felt, violent mobs would rise to destroy property. The working class, in Barnard's estimation, was "a mighty power, and there is a physical strength slumbering in their arms in peaceful times and a greater and more terrible than mere strength of muscles in their uninformed intellect and uninstructed heart, which is liable at any time to be called into exercise."[8]

Barnard was enlightened enough to recognize that elements inclined toward anarchy, revolution, and crime had some legitimate grievances. He believed that industrialism endangered the health of women and children, and he condemned the badly ventilated and poorly lighted slum dwellings. Also, he was aware that long, dull hours of work left the worker no time or energy to listen to sermons and lectures and often led him, craving excitement, to crime and drunkenness.

Barnard believed that social disturbances might best be avoided and the *status quo* maintained if sharp class distinctions were eliminated and, in Curti's words, if everyone could live in a society "where all ranks and occupations of men would enjoy the pleasure of taste and imagination, respectful manners and correct morals."[9] Opportunities should be provided for talented individuals among the poor to advance according to their ability, by way of education, though Barnard had no doubt that the great mass of urban workers' children would remain in the same class as their parents. Nevertheless, all could lead happy, decent lives and share in society's cultural values.

In Barnard's judgement, much class prejudice could be blamed on the structure of the educational system, carried over from colonial days, and especially the private schools. Private academies for the children of the wealthy, he was convinced, created class antagonism, for which reason he strongly advocated public high schools where the children of rich and poor could mingle. The private school is condemned by Barnard in the following statement, written for the *Journal of the Rhode Island Institute of Instruction*, in 1845:

It classifies society at the root, by assorting children according to the wealth, education, or outward circumstances of their parents into different schools; and educates children of the same neighborhood differently and unequally. These differences of culture, as to manners, morals, and intellectual tastes and habits, begun in childhood and strengthened by differences in occupation, which are determined mainly by early education, open a real chasm between members of the same society, broad and deep, which equal laws and political theories cannot close.[10]

Earlier, Barnard had expressed similar views, perhaps in even more emphatic terms, in an article for the *Connecticut Common School Journal*, in 1840:

The children who attend the private school at home, or go abroad to the academy or boarding school, associate almost of necessity together, and thus, with the enjoyment of superior advantages, and the influence of exclusive association, they grow up with a feeling of superiority every way at war with their own usefulness and the peace of society. On the other hand, the children of the district school feel more or less the depressing influences of their inferior advantages, and imbibe feelings of jealousy, if not of hostility, towards their more fortunate neighbors.[11]

Resentments toward the rich harbored by the poor could be substantially reduced if all children were to begin with a common educational foundation, enjoying equality of educational opportunity. The poor would then feel, according to Barnard, that "whatever may betide them, their children are born to an inheritance more valuable than lands or shops, in the free access to institutions where as good education can be had as money can buy at home or abroad."[12]

As noted elsewhere, in the chapter discussing educational finance, however, Barnard did not propose totally free schools. Children whose parents could afford to pay tuition beyond taxes would be expected to provide additional support for the public schools. Curti suggests that this plan could have defeated Barnard's purpose to break down class distinctions and prejudices. On the other hand, to offset this undemocratic scheme, Barnard urged a policy of larger state appropriations to the smaller and poorer school districts, and the establishment of scholarships for gifted students to attend college.

As important steps toward ameliorating the condition of the poor, Barnard proposed that the wealthy undertake a program of slum clearance, building model tenement houses for modest rentals; and construct attractive, well-planned schoolhouses with libraries, lecture rooms, and facilities for healthy, harmless amusements. At the same time, Barnard did not contemplate any fundamental reorganization of the economic system to allow the poor to share more equally in the nation's wealth, and thereby be better able to afford and enjoy the cultural advantages so highly rated by Barnard and his class. In part, this attitude can be traced to a belief in the uplifting effects of general public education, and no less to having been born and bred in a privileged segment of society that failed to perceive economic and other obstacles in the way of the poor. Curti remarks of Barnard, "With the limitations imposed on him by his own environment and associations he could not have been expected to see the force of the argument that the culture he so much valued, being a class culture, could not easily be imposed on a class which had not shared in creating it."[13] Beyond these factors was the traditional American individualism, which held that every person of worth was capable through his own efforts of rising to the top — the rags-to-riches theme preached by Horatio Alger to millions of American boys. Barnard, therefore, saw nothing unreasonable in the prevailing order of industrial capitalism. His philosophy, straight from Benjamin Franklin, was thus stated, as late as 1872:

In this country, the art of acquisition is pretty well understood; for which we are indebted, mainly to the necessities of a poor but intelligent ancestry, and the possession of rich but undeveloped material and facilities, but in no small degree to the maxims of POOR RICHARD, which, by household and schoolbook repetition, have become inwrought into the texture of every American mind.[14]

Though Barnard professed to be open-minded in inquiries into controversial subjects, articles published in the *American Journal of Education* and elsewhere were definitely slanted in favor of capitalistic theory, while contemporary socialistic movements were ignored. An example is an article entitled "Education, A Preventive of Misery and Crime," a prize essay from the British Schoolmasters' Association, demonstrating that the chief causes of poverty are extravagance, improvidence, drunkenness, tardiness, and ignorance.[15] A second article, "Elementary Instruction in Economical Science," maintains that education in political economy is a proper antidote to having workingmen organize and strike. If workers were taught basic economic truths, there would be an end to the chronic hostility between capitalists and laborers.[16]

Barnard did not condone ruthless behavior or ostentatious displays on the part of rich men, but he defended the pursuit of wealth, in part because it provided resources for philanthropy. Barnard frequently sought and was grateful to men of wealth for their benefactions to education. As president of St. John's College, he proposed to appoint to the board of directors donors who endowed chairs.

But if Barnard did not wish to change the existing economic order, he was without question a reformer in the field of education. Like Pestalozzi, he opposed the prevailing emphasis upon book

learning and urged more attention to the utilitarian disciplines in
the curriculum. Barnard urged instruction in whatever was practical and useful in the principles of health, agriculture, commerce,
and mechanics. The needs of the community were to be considered
paramount. An industrial society would be strengthened by teaching students to be hard-working, efficient, and frugal, as well as by
inculcating in them basic knowledge and moral virtues.

At the secondary school level, Barnard believed that high schools
and special institutions could be valuable aids to the nation's industries. He advocated an increase in the number of technical schools
and recommended that high schools teach "such studies as navigation, bookkeeping, surveying, botany, chemistry, and kindred
studies which are directly connected with success in the varied
departments of domestic and inland trade, with foreign commerce,
with gardening, with agriculture, the manufacturing and domestic
arts."[17]

Barnard was an American patriot. Though he believed that he
and his countrymen could derive valuable lessons from the European educational experience, he was equally convinced that
America should maintain its cultural independence from Europe.
Barnard never recommended adoption of old-world ideals and
practices without change. On the other hand, as Curti points out,
"In spite of his cultural patriotism, the fact that he devoted thousands of pages of the *American Journal of Education* to European
education must have helped to prolong our dependence on European example."[18]

Barnard was far less critical than Horace Mann in his evaluation
of American history and civilization. An example of the former's
uncritical acceptance of the "American mission" is quoted by
Curti from a Barnard manuscript prepared for a lecture: "Here on
these shores the claims of humanity in its broadest sense are recognized in the government under which we live. From the first hour
our history opened on the rock of Plymouth, all that gives value to
human life, security to human happiness, protection to personal
rights, to private property and public liberty has been wrought out
by the agency of institutions, created by and for the benefit of the
people themselves."[19] Unlike Mann, who gave history as a school

subject a low rating because of its emphasis on war, Barnard strongly supported the teaching of history and the study of state and national constitutions.

In political matters, Barnard was reasonably successful in maintaining a nonpartisan stance. Such an attitude was essential, he believed, to gain general support for the public schools and for educational reform. The wisdom of the policy was demonstrated by the wide backing which Barnard was able to enlist from the leading men of both political parties and from wealthy philanthropists for the reorganization and increased financial support of public education. The selection of teachers should be governed, Barnard declared, by the same principle of nonpartisanship. Elisha R. Potter, who succeeded Barnard as Rhode Island Commissioner of Education, in a letter to Governor Thomas of Maryland in 1867, testified that the latter was able to secure the support of all parties, who found it possible to work harmoniously together under his unselfish and enthusiastic leadership, putting aside their usual prejudices and antagonisms.

Nevertheless, as has been indicated, Barnard was not neutral toward many important issues of his day. In the sphere of educational and social philosophy, he was a conservative. He believed in the maintenance of the capitalist system and shared the belief of patriotic Americans in general that America was the best place in which to have been born and to live. Barnard's principal contributions to the educational world were his popularization of the free school idea, his educational journalism, his advocacy of functional education, and his crusade to extend educational opportunities to the underprivileged.

CHAPTER 13

Influence on American Education

INFLUENCE is usually intangible and difficult to measure, but the impact of Henry Barnard on American educational development in the nineteenth century is traceable in a variety of ways. His achievements in Connecticut and Rhode Island were of lasting significance in those states, and, serving as models, spread in widening circles from New England to the South and West and even to Europe and Latin America.

Barnard's counsel and help were given freely in all parts of the country. He was an effective speaker and during his wide travels his faith in and enthusiasm for education awakened a similar response wherever he went. From his early years, he recognized the great need for enlightening the public, especially those associated with the schools, and this he accomplished by extensive correspondence, public addresses, and, most of all, by his writing and publishing.

An American educational historian, Edgar W. Knight, has traced Barnard influence in the South.[1] Knight discovered documentary evidence that the commissioners of free schools in Charleston, South Carolina, appointed a school principal because he was "particularly recommended to the Committee by Mr. Barnard who is so well known to the Public in connection with works on education."[2] Thereafter, Barnard frequently exchnged letters with the principal, J. D. Geddings, on the progress of the Charleston schools. Another correspondent was William H. Stiles, Speaker of the House of the Georgia Legislature. Writing in 1856, when the legislature was in session and had under consideration the establishment of a system of common schools, Stiles wrote to Barnard that he was

poring over Barnard's "National Education in Europe" & "Normal Schools" "Report relating to the Public Schools of Rhode Island" "Annual

110

Report of the Superintendent of Common Schools in Connecticut"
"Principles of School Architecture" & "Journal of Education" and I
cannot refrain from saying that I should give most anything if I only had
Mr. Barnard by my side for a half hour to aid me in preparing a bill for the
adoption of a system of Common Schools to our most extensive but for
the greater part sparsely settled country.[3]

A South Carolina educator, Christopher Gustavus Memminger,
wrote in 1856 to express appreciation to Barnard for "the greatest
interest that you take in our efforts to set our State aright in the
proper road to general education." Memminger noted that the
Southerners were irritated "by the taunts and abuse of many
Northern newspapers and politicians, yet they continue to estimate
aright the benefits conferred upon our whole people by such men
as yourself." There was considerable opposition, Memminger reported, to plans for the improvement of public education, and he
requested Barnard to supply arguments and material to strengthen
the cause of common schools.[4]

From Selma, Alabama, A. W. Richardson wrote to Barnard on
March 23, 1857: "Being one of the few professional teachers of
Alabama whose locks have grown grey in the service, I feel a strong
desire to become a subscriber for your ably-conducted, and most
excellent Journal. I have read, with great satisfaction, a few stray
numbers of your noble quarterly." Concerning the current state of
education in Alabama, Richardson added:

The cause of Education is inspiring renewed interest among our people.
They are becoming pretty thoroughly convinced that we must either build
up schools and colleges, or expend an *equal,* if not a much greater *amount*
in erecting jails and penitentiaries. Leviathan must in some way be *sub-
dued.* If we cannot transform him into a rational creature, then, must
chains and a prisonhouse restrain the native malignity of his disposition.[5]

From Texas, Ashbel Smith, a fellow Yale graduate, wrote to Barnard, on July 6, 1858, about a new school building in Houston.
"Next comes the business of its furniture," Smith stated. "I have
given the Trustees your School architecture and some numbers of
your Journal of Education. Some of our merchants, who are also

trustees of the school will go to the North in a short time, and will there I presume make the purchases of the furniture."[6] Smith had been elected superintendent of the school, contrary to his wishes, and asked Barnard's advice about accepting the post for more than a temporary appointment.

Few of Barnard's replies to his admirers and correspondents in the South have been preserved, while Barnard meticulously filed away letters and papers received by him. The record is therefore one-sided and the complete story of Barnard's influence on Southern education cannot be told.

An Illinois superintendent of schools, Newton C. Dougherty, in an article for the National Educational Association's *Journal of Proceedings and Addresses,* 1901, described "The Influence of Henry Barnard on Schools in the West."[7] In the mid-nineteenth century, according to Dougherty, the schools in the Western states were in acute need of stronger financial support. Beyond that fact, however, the educators of the region needed information as to what had been accomplished elsewhere in promoting education, and, further, the information should be put in such form as to act as a powerful stimulus to the educational forces. "How admirably adapted," stated Dougherty, "was Barnard's *Journal* to supply both these wants!" In the *Journal,* Dougherty pointed out, the Western teachers found a treasury of educational history and methods, descriptions of prevailing systems, educational philosophy, practical guidance for inexperienced teachers, and a constant source of inspiration.

Dougherty did not maintain that the *Journal* and Barnard's other writings were read by numerous school officers and teachers in the Western states. He pointed out, instead, that Barnard's ideas and general philosophy were assimilated by enlightened leaders and transmitted through them to educational meetings, to teachers' institutes, and to normal and other schools. The end result, Dougherty concluded, was to aid the educational reformers, gain acceptance for new ideas by the people at large, increase the number and quality of the schools, promote the establishment of normal schools, improve schoolhouses, and increase expenditures for public education.[8]

Convincing documentary proof exists to show that the influence of Barnard's *American Journal of Education* was significant among diverse groups of educators. A detailed study of the *Journal's* distribution and use was undertaken by Richard Emmons Thursfield.[9] An examination of Barnard's surviving correspondence reveals that subscribers to the *Journal* included state superintendents of public instruction, college teachers, normal school principals, principals of academies, seminaries, high schools, and grammar schools, city superintendents of schools, leaders in the public school movement, college presidents, prominent lay persons interested in education, and teachers.

Among state school superintendents, Thursfield found that fifteen of thirty-one states were represented on the subscription list — a substantial percentage in view of the fact that in most instances the superintendents were political appointees, and therefore unlikely to have strong professional motivations. No state superintendent south of the Mason and Dixon Line ordered the *Journal* before 1866. John Swett, dynamic young builder of California's school system, reported in 1856 that a large number of copies had "found their way out here" and were being read with keen interest.[10] John M. Gregory, superintendent of public schools of Michigan (later president of the University of Illinois), wrote to Barnard: "I shall of course wish a copy for the office and another copy for my own library and will endeavor to get some other names to send with my own."[11] The evidence is reasonably conclusive that the more professional-minded state superintendents wanted the *Journal* and frequently were willing to pay for it out of their own pockets if no state funds were available.

Leaders among the evolving profession of city school superintendents also found the *Journal* of practical value and used it in their work. John D. Philbrick, Boston's second superintendent of schools, often referred to the *Journal* during his twenty years in that office and arranged to purchase sets for the Boston schools. As a member of an international jury at the 1873 Vienna Exposition, Philbrick was instrumental in obtaining a Medal of Merit for Barnard in recognition of his "great labors and sacrifices in publishing the *American Journal of Education*."[12] A New York superintendent, N. A. Calkin, a popularizer of Pestalozzian ideas, expressed the opinion that the *Journal* was "the most valuable of all collections of educational literature."[13] Andrew J. Rickoff, Cleveland superintendent, acknowledged his indebtedness to the *Journal*, stating, "I found it invaluable in making reply to Mr. Hinsdale's attack on 'Our Common Schools.'"[14] St. Louis' influential superintendent, William T. Harris, aided in obtaining a wider distribution of the *Journal* and later helped to relieve Barnard's financial problems by leading a movement to save the printing plates. There appears to be a close correlation between the addresses delivered to teachers' gatherings by leading superintendents and subscribers to the *Journal,* i.e., these individuals relied heavily upon the *Journal* as a source for their speeches, reports, and published works.

Prominent principals of academies, private seminaries, and different types of high schools were on the *Journal's* subscription list. A complete set was ordered by H. B. Lawrence of the Appleton Street School at Holyoke, and after the volumes had been in his school for about a year, Lawrence wrote:

Our eleven teachers, holding weekly meetings for the discussion of educational questions, have studied and consulted these twenty-eight volumes nearly every week since the purchase.... Our year's study has improved our methods, given us broader and more correct views of education, and increased our love of the profession. The improvement of our schools has been very marked. We are free to acknowledge that this change is largely due to the influence of Dr. Barnard's *Journal.*[15]

A group that Barnard particularly desired to reach with the *Journal* was normal school principals and teachers, to aid teacher-education programs being developed in these newly created schools. The records show that the *Journal* was available in many of the more important normal schools and in college and university libraries where chairs of pedagogy or courses for teachers were established. If their governing boards were unable or unwilling to purchase sets, the principals were likely to subscribe personally.

Another key group toward whom Barnard directed his aim was

college and university presidents and professors. A special effort was made to provide a convenient synthesis of materials in the *Journal* relating to their interests. Thursfield notes that "the editor of the *Journal* was highly respected by some of the most distinguished college presidents who were charting new courses in the field of higher education. They consulted him and honored his views."[16] An extensive correspondence has been preserved between Henry Barnard and President Frederick Barnard of Columbia (for whom Barnard College is named). The letters show that President Barnard turned to the *Journal* often as he struggled with such problems as classical versus scientific studies, the meaning of a liberal education, elective studies, and the place of the extra-collegiate schools in the making of an American university.

Few teachers subscribed to the *Journal,* at least in part for financal reasons, because of their niggardly salaries, and also no doubt because it was not sufficiently popular in tone. An educational publisher, C. W. Bardeen of Syracuse, concluded that "the number of teachers capable of appreciating such reading will always be small."[17] Nevertheless, an occasional teacher was aware of the periodical's value. For example, J. V. N. Standish of Galesburg, Illinois, wrote in 1860, "Of all the books in my library, I prize Barnard's *American Journal of Education* the *most.* It is a woik, it seems to me, that a teacher of *any character as a teacher,* cannot do without."[18]

Much evidence supports the belief that the *Journal* had wide influence upon leaders in American education during its period of publication. There was a close connection between the list of *Journal* subscribers and the recognized educational leadership of the nation. Those who rose to top positions in various kinds of educational institutions and endeavor subscribed to and read the *Journal* throughout their careers. It should be noted also that the publication's geographical distribution was extraordinarily wide, in the United States and abroad. A reasonable conclusion, therefore, is that the *Journal* had influence, much of it perhaps indirect, quite out of proportion to the number of subscribers.

The availability of the *Journal* was enhanced for non-individual subscribers by its presence in libraries. Sets were to be found on the shelves of the most important public, school, college, and university libraries at home and abroad. To encourage institutional subscriptions, Barnard offered special discounts. College libraries too poor to purchase sets received them through donations from philanthropic individuals. One of the largest groups of subscribers was normal school libraries.

The influence and recognition of the *Journal* abroad can be measured to some extent by the list of subscribers and frequent references to it by foreign educators. The foreign circulation of the *Journal* was greater than most nineteenth-century American periodicals. Thursfield refers to "the obstructive tactics of English book agents toward American books" which made difficult the procurement of such material as the *Journal* and Barnard's "Library of Education." Despite the obstacles, sets were placed in the principal libraries of England and Scotland and were received by leading individual educators. Tributes to the value of his work were also received by Barnard from Austria, Germany, France, Belgium, Italy, Switzerland, Canada, Chile, and Argentina.

Long after the *American Journal of Education* ceased publication, in 1881, and indeed until the present day, it has continued to be a valuable record of all aspects of early American educational development. Among the areas in which it has remained a primary source of information are the beginnings of kindergarten, technical, and scientific schools, special education, the education of blacks, college and university instruction, curricula, and methodology, the education of delinquent children, secondary education, and the education of women. In these and other subjects, Barnard's contributions to the literature were often trailblazing, opening up new fields to the educational world. While U.S. Commissioner of Education, Barnard laid down certain guidelines which subsequently had permanent influence on the nature of the Bureau's publications.

Later historians of education have drawn extensively upon the *Journal* and Barnard's other work — notably Ellwood P. Cubberley, Paul Monroe, Frederick Eby, Charles Flinn Arrowood, and Robert Ulich, all of whom acknowledged their indebtedness to Barnard. Educational journalism in America, especially soon after

Barnard, was also shaped to a significant degree by the standards that he established. Outstanding instances are G. Stanley Hall's *Pedagogical Seminary,* Nicholas Murray Butler's *Educational Review,* and J. McKeen Cattell's *School and Society.*

CHAPTER 14

Afterword

HENRY Barnard's life spanned almost the entire nineteenth century. Crowded into those years was a phenomenal range of activities, marked by many notable achievements. Barnard was the first secretary of the Connecticut Board of Commissioners of Common Schools; founder and editor of the *Connecticut Common School Journal,* from which the modern-day *Connecticut Teacher* is descended; the first State Superintendent of Education in Rhode Island; first to hold the position of Superintendent of Common Schools of Connecticut, concurrently with being the first principal of the New Britain State Normal School (now Central Connecticut State College); Chancellor of the University of Wisconsin; President of St. John's College, Maryland; first United States Commissioner of Education; and founder and editor of the *American Journal of Education* from 1856 to 1882.

Barnard's contributions to the expansion, development, and improvement of education in the United States were manifold. Wherever the need was apparent, he threw himself with indefatigable energy into correcting conditions.

The chief areas in which Barnard concentrated his efforts were the improvement of the teaching profession; the levying of adequate local school taxes; the building of schoolhouses with proper attention to light, heating, ventilation, furnishing, and decoration; the establishment of school libraries; and better and more uniform textbooks and teaching apparatus. Barnard was determined "that the common school should no longer be regarded as common because it is cheap, inferior, and attended only by the poor and those who are indifferent to the education of their children, but *common* as the sunshine and the air, because its blessings are open to all and enjoyed by all."[1]

Barnard has rightly been termed the "Father of Teacher Education in America." His annual reports for Connecticut and Rhode Island depicted the plight of the teacher in the district school. At the outset, he stated, "facts are what we need and the sooner we can procure them the sooner shall we be able to carry forward with efficiency our system of common school instruction."[2] Some teachers had been educated in academies and female seminaries, but in many instances their training had been even more elementary. As Barnard viewed the situation, the chief task was to convert "school keeping" into "school teaching." His attack on the problem took the form of innumerable speeches, of demonstrations, of model schools and model teachers, as well as the printed word. He organized institutes for teachers, convinced the public of the need for normal schools, and encouraged the introduction of new teaching methods developed in Europe by Comenius, Ratke, Basedow, and Pestalozzi.

When Barnard finally had an opportunity to organize and establish a full-fledged normal school, he was guided by certain principles based on actual experience and prolonged study. First, he had to choose between attaching his teacher-training institution to one of the existing colleges in Connecticut or setting up a separate institution. He chose the second plan, for, he asserted, "In no state in Europe has the experiment of making seminaries for primary school teachers an appendage to a university or gymnasium or any other school of an academic character proven successful."[3] Second was the matter of location. The normal school, Barnard felt, should be placed as near the seat of government as possible: "The interests of popular education in each state demand the establishment, at the seat of government and under the patronage of the legislature, of a normal school."[4] A third point was standards for admission, defined by Barnard as good health, a vigorous and buoyant constitution and lively, cheerful spirits; good manners; a love of and sympathy with children; and adequate talent and basic education. In Barnard's opinion, a normal school without a model school — pupils for the student teachers to practice upon — was like a shoemaker's shop without leather; such a unit has been a standard feature of teacher-training institutions since his day.

From a practical point of view, one of Barnard's most significant achievements was to bring about improved housing for the public schools. The prevailing situation was described by Horace Mann, who wrote: "In 1837 not one-third of the public schoolhouses of Massachusetts would have been considered tenantable by any decent family out of the poorhouse or in it."[5] And Superintendent Samuel Young wrote of the public schools of New York: "Only one-third of the whole number of schoolhouses visited were found in good repair; another third in ordinary and comfortable condition only in this respect — in other words, barely sufficient for the convenience and accommodation of the teachers and pupils; while the remainder, consisting of 3319, were to all intents and purposes unfit for the reception of man or beast."[6] When Barnard completed five years in Rhode Island, good schoolhouses had largely replaced such buildings as those described in Massachusetts and New York, and later his missionary zeal achieved similar results in Connecticut. Also highly influential everywhere were the various editions of his *School Architecture*.

Barnard was instrumental in extending the scope of the common school to include secondary education. He saw that the times demanded teaching beyond the strictly elementary, that is, such skills and knowledge to aid in national development as navigation, surveying, bookkeeping, and local, state, and national history. The public high school, Barnard recognized, was the kind of institution required to meet the needs. Not without justification, the high school has been characterized as the greatest of American social inventions, an institution where children of all faiths, all races, and all social background learn to work and play together.

The status of women in society and in the educational world was one of Barnard's primary concerns throughout his career. Writing in 1840, he philosophized:

And how without books as the grand means of intellectual cultivation, are the daughters of the State to obtain that knowledge on a thousand subjects, which is so desirable in the character of a female, as well as so essential to the discharge of the duties to which she is destined? Young men, it may be said, have a larger circle of action; they are more in promiscuous society, at least they have a far wider range of business occupations, all of which stimulate thought, suggest inquiry and furnish means for improvement. But the sphere of females is domestic. Their life is comparatively secluded. . . . [I]f at the same time she is debarred from access to books, by what means, through what channels, is she to obtain the knowledge so indispensable for the fit discharge of maternal and domestic duties, and for rendering herself an enlightened companion for intelligent man? Without books, except in cases of extraordinary natural endowment, she will be doomed to relative ignorance and incapacity.[7]

Like Horace Mann in Massachusetts, Barnard urged the employment of more women teachers in the schools. At the beginning of his educational career, women were just emerging from the shelter of their homes to teach in the poorly regarded, neglected summer schools. Barnard's insistence upon bringing a larger number of women into the school system was based on pedagogical and economic grounds. In his judgment, women were better qualified than men in character and disposition for some phases of work in the schools and equally endowed in mental ability. Barnard believed that the primary grades should be staffed exclusively by women teachers, while the high schools should have both men and women teachers. As proof of the merit of his arguments, Barnard pointed out that the "introduction of a large number of female teachers, in winter as well as in summer, has greatly improved the discipline, moral influence, and *manners* of the Rhode Island public schools."[8]

The modern survey of education owes its origin to Henry Barnard to a greater extent than to any other individual. Barnard was appointed by Governor James Fenner of Rhode Island to make the first survey of a state public school system. The assignment was in thorough accord with the former's temperament and educational philosophy. Barnard was convinced that any advance in education hinged upon a collection of facts. Accordingly, "the young man with a notebook" became a familiar figure in Rhode Island and Connecticut schools. In his investigations, Barnard used most of the methods of inquiry recognized in modern survey practices, and his reports could serve as models for surveys today in their presentation of facts and statistics.

Barnard was also a firm believer in a national system of education and of a major role for the federal government in the nation's educational affairs. As the first U.S. Commissioner of Education, he attempted to make this concept a reality but was continually frustrated by local, state and regional jealousies and by political interference. Not until the second half of the twentieth century did American educators have a direct voice at the cabinet level of government, except in such specialized areas as agriculture and federal land grants. The 1867 bill creating a Department of Education was quickly aborted. Barnard was successful, however, in initiating the compilation and publication of educational statistics for the whole country, a series which became a permanent feature of the Bureau of Education's responsibilities.

As visualized by Barnard, a central agency for the advancement of education in the United States should be headed by a secretary, who would have the following duties, in order to increase and diffuse knowledge on educational matters, especially popular education: collect and make available for use information on advances in educational theory and practice in all states and countries; edit educational books and journals; collect plans and models of schoolhouses and furniture, maps and other educational materials, and educational reports and documents from all states and countries; institute a system of educational exchange between literary institutions in the United States and other countries; and submit an annual report on the progress of education at home and abroad. Thus was projected a blueprint for the future followed in most important respects by Barnard's successors.

Henry Barnard's publications, and especially the monumental *American Journal of Education,* are of permanent significance. Richard K. Morris, in writing of "The Barnard Legacy," declares that the *Journal* "stands today as a classic repository of educational history, catholic in scope, scholarly in treatment — in short, the greatest single encyclopedia of world-wide topics on education and related subjects compiled by one man."[9] In the *Journal* and other publications, Barnard set a high standard for educational literature.

After his frequently disappointing experiences in public offices, Barnard clearly lost any taste that he may have originally had for politics, and thenceforth his interests were centered on educational literature.

Historians of education are in general agreement that four names stand out among the founders of modern public education: Heinrich Pestalozzi, Friedrich Froebel, Horace Mann, and Henry Barnard. Each built on the work of his predecessors, and at the same time made his own unique contributions. In America, Barnard's name will always be linked with Horace Mann's as one who aroused public interest in education, and convinced the educational world of the need for professionally trained teachers, proper schoolhouses and educational equipment, and of the importance of educational literature and broadly-based courses of study.

The philosophy which motivated Henry Barnard throughout his career is eloquently expressed in his own words: "The education of a people bears a constant and most pre-eminently influential relation to its attainments and excellences — physical, mental, and moral.... [T]he history of education affords the only ready and perfect key to the history of the human race, and of each nation in it, — an unfailing standard for estimating its advance or retreat upon the line of human progress."[10]

Notes and References

Chapter One

1. Letter from Jonathan Lam to Henry Barnard, Feb. 2, 1844 (Monroe Collection).
2. Letter to Barnard, July 31, 1845 (Monroe Collection).
3. *American Journal of Education,* 1 (1856), p. 663.
4. Clifton, John L. *Famous American Educators* (Columbus, Ohio, 1933), p. 28.
5. Jenkins, R. C. *Henry Barnard* (Hartford, Conn., 1937), p. 12.
6. Steiner, Bernard C. *Life of Henry Barnard* (Wash., D.C., 1919), pp. 8-9. (U.S. Bureau of Education *Bulletin,* 1919, No. 8).
7. Jenkins, *op. cit.,* pp. 14-15.
8. *New England Magazine,* N.S. 14 (1896), p. 563.
9. *American Journal of Education,* 1 (1856), p. 604.
10. Letter of James Lowrey, April 18, 1831 (Monroe Collection).
11. Steiner, *op. cit.,* p. 24.
12. Monroe, Will S. *Educational Labors of Henry Barnard* (Syracuse, 1893), p. 9.
13. *American Journal of Education,* 28 (1878), p. 227.

Chapter Two

1. Monroe, *op. cit.,* pp. 10-11.
2. Jenkins, *op. cit.,* p. 27.
3. *Ibid.,* p. 29.
4. Monroe, *op. cit.,* pp. 11-12.
5. Jenkins, *op. cit.,* p. 30.
6. *Ibid.*
7. *Ibid.,* p. 59. Monroe, *op. cit.,* p. 14.
8. Jenkins, *op. cit.,* p. 59.
9. Steiner, *op. cit.,* p. 78.
10. U.S. Commissioner of Education, *Report,* 1896-97, v. 1, p. 795.
11. Jenkins, *op. cit.,* p. 61.
12. *Ibid.*

Chapter Three

1. Steiner, *op. cit.*, p. 54.
2. *Ibid.*
3. *Ibid.*
4. *Ibid.*, p. 55.
5. Jenkins, *op. cit.*, p. 37.
6. *Ibid.*, p. 41.
7. *American Journal of Education,* 1 (1856), p. 729.
8. *Ibid.*, p. 730.
9. *Ibid.*
10. *Ibid.*
11. *Ibid.*
12. *Ibid.*, p. 733.
13. *Ibid.*
14. Monroe, *op. cit.*, p. 16.

Chapter Four

1. Panzer, Conrad E. *Public Education in Wisconsin* (Madison, Wis., 1924), p. 112.
2. U.S. Commissioner of Education, *Report,* 1896-97, p. 802.
3. Unpublished letter to Daniel Coil Gilman, Nov. 4, 1858 (Monroe Collection, New York University).
4. Unpublished letter to Daniel Coit Gilman, October 29, 1859 (Monroe Collection, New York University).
5. U.S. Commissioner of Education, *Report,* 1896-97, p. 802.
6. Blair, Anna Lou. *Henry Barnard* (Minneapolis, 1938), p. 69.
7. *Ibid.*, p. 67.
8. U.S. Commissioner of Education, *Report,* 1896-97, p. 803.
9. Blair, *op. cit.*, p. 172.
10. Steiner, *op. cit.*, p. 93.
11. Jenkins, *op. cit.*, p. 66.
12. Blair, *op. cit.*, p. 193.

Chapter Five

1. Letter in Gilman Papers, John Hopkins University.
2. *Scientific Monthly,* 36 (1933), p. 121.
3. *Ibid.*, p. 122.
4. *Ibid.*

5. *Ibid.,* p. 123.

6. *Connecticut Quarterly,* 4 (1898), p. 133.

7. National Education Association, *Addresses and Proceedings,* 1901, p. 410.

8. U.S. Secreatary of the Interior, *Annual Report.* (Wash., D.C., 1868), p. v-vi.

9. Blair, *op. cit.,* p. 79.

10. *Ibid.,* p. 82.

11. NEA, *Addresses, op. cit.,* p. 414.

Chapter Six

1. *American Journal of Education,* 1 (1856), pp. 1-2.

2. *Ibid.,* p. 1.

3. Thursfield, Richard E. *Henry Barnard's American Journal of Education* (Baltimore, 1945), 359 pp.

4. *Ibid.,* p. 93.

5. *Ibid.,* p. 97.

6. *American Journal of Education,* 8 (1860), pp. 371-82.

7. *Ibid.,* pp. 382-402.

8. *Ibid.,* 11 (1862), pp. 563-72.

9. Thursfield, *op. cit.,* p. 153.

10. *Ibid.,* p. 154.

11. *American Journal of Education,* 8 (1860), p. 320.

12. Monroe, *op. cit.,* p. 33.

13. *Ibid.*

14. *Westminster Review,* 65 (1856), p. 141.

15. *North American Review,* 122 (1870), p. 193.

Chapter Seven

1. *American Journal of Education,* 1 (1856), pp. 660-61.

2. *Ibid.,* p. 661.

3. *Ibid.,* p. 662.

4. *Ibid.*

5. *History of Education Quarterly,* 11 (1971), p. 41.

6. *Ibid.*

7. National Education Association, *Addresses and Proceedings,* 1901, p. 393.

8. *Ibid.,* p. 393.

9. Panzer, *op. cit.,* p. 245.

10. Jenkins, *op. cit.,* p. 54.

11. Brubacher, John S. *Henry Barnard on Education* (N.Y., 1931), pp. 168-69.

12. Blair, *op. cit.,* p. 232.

13. Brubacher, *op. cit.,* p. 176.

14. *Ibid.,* p. 177.

15. Jenkins, *op. cit.,* p. 45.

16. Thursfield, *op. cit.,* p. 244.

17. Blair, *op. cit.,* p. 237.

Chapter Eight

1. Jenkins, *op. cit.,* p. 21.

2. *American Journal of Education,* 4 (1858), p. 149.

3. Thursfield, *op. cit.,* p. 138.

4. *Ibid.,* p. 153.

5. *Ibid.,* p. 154.

6. *Ibid.,* p. 182.

Chapter Nine

1. Barnard, Henry. *School Architecture,* 6th ed. (N.Y., 1860), p. 7.

2. *Ibid.*

3. Barnard, Henry. *Report on the Condition and Improvement of the Public Schools of Rhode Island* (Providence, 1845), pp. 50-51.

4. *Ibid.,* p. 59.

5. *Ibid.,* p. 61.

6. Barnard, Henry. *First Annual Report as Secretary to the Board of Commissioners of Common Schools in Connecticut* (Hartford, 1839), pp. 41-43.

7. *Ibid., Second Annual Report* (Hartford, 1840), pp. 29-33.

8. *Ibid., Third Annual Report* (Hartford, 1841), pp. 26-27.

9. *American Journal of Education,* 10 (1861), pp. 517-20.

10. Barnard, *Second Annual Report,* pp. 14-19.

11. *Ibid.,* pp. 26-29.

12. Barnard, *Report on the Condition and Improvement of the Public Schools of Rhode Island,* p. 34.

13. *Ibid.,* p. 38.

14. *Ibid.,* p. 39.

15. Barnard, *First Annual Report,* pp. 15-21.

Chapter Ten

1. Connecticut Board of Commissioners of Common Schools, *Seventh Annual Report* (Hartford, 1852), pp. 36-37.
2. U.S. Commissioner of Education, *Report,* 1896-97. (Wash., D.C., 1898), p. 774.
3. Jenkins, *op. cit.,* p. 39.
4. Connecticut Board of Commissioners of Common Schools, *Seventh Annual Report,* p. 36.
5. *Connecticut Common School Journal,* 1 (1838), p. 162.
6. *Ibid.,* p. 173.
7. Connecticut Board of Commissioners of Common Schools, *Annual Report.* (Hartford, 1842), p. 25.
8. *Ibid.,* 1850, pp. 25-32.
9. Mead, A.R. "Henry Barnard and Free Schools," *Educational Administration and Supervision,* 31 (1945), p. 551.
10. Connecticut Board of Commissioners of Common Schools, *Annual Report* (Hartford, 1853), pp. 169-71.
11. *Connecticut Common School Journal,* 10 (1855), p. 310.
12. Mead, *op. cit.,* p. 552.
13. *Ibid.,* p. 553.

Chapter Eleven

1. Jenkins, *op. cit.,* pp. 14-15.
2. *Ibid.,* p. 15.
3. *Ibid.,* pp. 71-72.
4. *American Journal of Education,* 31 (1881), p. 369.
5. *Ibid.*
6. *Ibid.*, p. 373.
7. Jenkins, *op. cit.,* p. 75.
8. *American Journal of Education,* 15 (1865), p. 307.
9. *Ibid.,* 1 (1856), p. 370.
10. *Ibid.*
11. Brubacher, *op. cit.,* p. 133.
12. *Ibid.,* p. 134.
13. *Ibid.,* p. 169.
14. *Ibid.,* p. 134.
15. *Ibid.,* p. 136.

Chapter Twelve

1. Curti, Merle, *The Social Ideas of American Educators* (N.Y., 1935), p. 139.

2. *American Journal of Education,* 8 (1860), p. 409.

3. Curti, *op. cit.*

4. *American Journal of Education,* 11 (1862), pp. 313-14.

5. Curti, *op. cit.,* p. 143.

6. *Ibid.,* p. 145.

7. *Ibid.*

8. *Ibid.,* p. 146.

9. *Ibid.,* p. 147.

10. *Journal of the Rhode Island Institute of Instruction,* 1 (1845), p. 38.

11. *Connecticut Common School Journal,* 2 (1840), p. 215.

12. Connecticut State Superintendent of Schools, *Report* (Hartford, 1850), p. 31.

13. Curti, *op. cit.,* p. 152.

14. *American Journal of Education,* 23 (1872), p. 249.

15. *Ibid.,* 11 (1862), pp. 77-93.

16. *Ibid.,* 10 (1861), pp. 105-15.

17. Connecticut State Superintendent of Schools, *Report* (Hartford, 1850), p. 28.

18. Curti, *op. cit.,* p. 161.

19. *Ibid.,* p. 162.

Chapter Thirteen

1. Knight, Edgar W. "Some Evidence of Henry Barnard's Influence in the South," *Educational Forum,* 13 (1949), pp. 301-12.

2. *Ibid.,* p. 303.

3. *Ibid.,* p. 308.

4. *Ibid.,* p. 309.

5. *Ibid.,* p. 310.

6. *Ibid.,* p. 311.

7. National Educational Association, *Addresses and Proceedings,* 1901, pp. 395-400.

8. *Ibid.,* p. 400.

9. Thursfield, *op. cit.,* pp. 268-315.

10. *Ibid.,* p. 272.

11. *Ibid.,* p. 273.

12. *Ibid.,* p. 275.

13. *Ibid.*
14. *Ibid.,* p. 276.
15. *Ibid.,* p. 280.
16. *Ibid.,* p. 285.
17. *Ibid.,* p. 287.
18. *Ibid.*

Chapter Fourteen

1. National Educational Association, *Addresses and Proceedings,* 1901, p. 401.

2. Morris, Richard K. "The Barnard Legacy," *School and Society,* 89 (1961), p. 394.

3. *School and Society,* 47 (1938), p. 343.

4. *Ibid.*

5. *Journal of the National Education Association,* 24 (1935), p. 234.

6. *Ibid.*

7. *Connecticut Common School Journal,* 2 (1840), pp. 191-92.

8. Jenkins, *op. cit.,* p. 45.

9. Morris, *op. cit.,* p. 394-95.

10. Barnard, Henry. "Introduction" to L. P. Brockett's *History and Progress of Education* (N.Y., 1866), p. 17.

Selected Bibliography

PRIMARY SOURCES

The principal collection of Henry Barnard papers is held by the New York University Library, Washington Square. Included are approximately 12,000 letters, chiefly written to Barnard and relating to business matters, such as the editing and publishing of the several journals with which Barnard was associated.

Another important collection is in the Watkinson Library, Trinity College, Hartford, Connecticut, which also holds Barnard's personal library and collection of American schoolbooks. Other collections are in the Hartford Historical Society, Wisconsin State Historical Society, University of Wisconsin, St. John's College (Minutes of the Board of Visitors and Governors of St. John's College, 1866), Connecticut State Department of Education, Hartford (Record of the Board of Trustees of the State Normal School, 1850–1864), and U.S. Office of Education, Washington, D.C.

Other valuable primary sources include Barnard's annual reports as Secretary of the Board of Commissioners of Common Schools, 1839–42, and as Superintendent of Common Schools in Connecticut, 1850–53; similar reports for Rhode Island; and files of the *American Journal of Education, Connecticut Common School Journal,* and the *Journal of the Rhode Island Institute of Instruction.*

SECONDARY SOURCES

BLAIR, ANNA LOU. *Henry Barnard, School Administrator.* Minneapolis: Educational Publishers, 1938. 294 pp. (Bibliography, pp. 283-94). A Yale University doctoral dissertation dealing comprehensively with all stages and aspects of Barnard's career, using historical and analytical methods.

BRUBACHER, JOHN S., ed., *Henry Barnard on Education.* N.Y.: McGraw-Hill, 1931. 298 pp. Primarily a highly selected anthology of Barnard's voluminous writings, designed to illustrate his views on education in general, sociological aspects, and such special topics as grading of schools, methods of instruction, the curriculum, teachers, and educational administration.

133

HARRIS, WILLIAM T., ed. "Henry Barnard." In *U.S. Report of the Commissioner of Education for 1902.* Wash., D.C.: Govt. Print. Off., 1903, pp. 887-926. A series of articles concerning several phases of Barnard's long career: "Henry Barnard's Services to Education in Connecticut," by W. T. Harris; "Henry Barnard as First U.S. Commissioner of Education," by A. D. Mayo; and "Establishment of the Office of the Commissioner of Education of the United States, and Henry Barnard's Relation to It," by W. T. Harris.

JENKINS, RALPH C. *Henry Barnard, an Introduction.* Hartford: Connecticut State Teachers Association, 1937. 118 pp. A general biography of Barnard by a Connecticut educator, president of the Danbury (Conn.) State Teachers College, 1935-46.

MAYO, AMORY D. "Henry Barnard." In *Report of the Commissioner of Education for 1896-97.* Wash., D.C.: Govt. Print. Office, 1898, pp. 769-810. A brief review of Barnard's life and educational contributions, with emphasis on his work in Connecticut and Rhode Island and as editor of the *American Journal of Education.*

Memorial Addresses. In: National Educational Association, *Journal of Proceedings and Addresses,* 40 (1901), 390-438. Contents: "Henry Barnard's Influence on the Establishment of Normal Schools in the United States," by Eliphalet Oram Lyle; "The Influence of Henry Barnard on Schools in the West," by Newton C. Dougherty; "Henry Barnard's Home Life and Influence Upon Education as Commissioner of Connecticut and Rhode Island," by Charles H. Keyes; "Henry Barnard as an Educational Critic," by Francis W. Parker; "Establishment of the Office of the Commissioner of Education of the United States, and Henry Barnard's Relation to It," by William T. Harris.

MONROE, WILL S. *The Educational Labors of Henry Barnard; a Study in the History of American Pedgagy.* Syracuse, N.Y.: C. W. Bardeen, 1893. 35 pp. (Bibliography, pp. 32-35). A sketch of Barnard's career by a leading contemporary educator, author, and close personal friend, whose extensive collection of Barnard's papers, now in New York University Library, is a primary source for biographers and students. A more complete biography written by Monroe was destroyed by fire before publication.

PORTER, NOAH. "Henry Barnard, His Labors in Connecticut and Rhode Island." *American Journal of Education,* 1 (1856), 659-738. The earliest general biography of Barnard, written by his classmate at

Yale, later president of Yale University (1871–86). Originally published in the *Connecticut Common School Journal,* January 1855.

STEINER, BERNARD C. *Life of Henry Barnard, the First United States Commissioner of Education, 1867-1870.* Wash., D.C.: Govt. Print. Office, 1919. 131 pp. (U.S. Bureau of Education Bulletin, 1919, No. 8). Written by a teacher, librarian, and historian, stressing Barnard's short and somewhat stormy stay in Washington.

THURSFIELD, RICHARD M. *American Journal of Education.* Baltimore: Johns Hopkins Press, 1945. 359 pp. (Johns Hopkins University Studies in Historical and Political Science, Ser. 63, No. 1). A definitive study of the monumental journal edited by Barnard from 1855 to 1881. Analyzes such matters as establishment and financing; editorial policy, scope, and scholarship; the journal as a record of American and European education; professional leadership and services; and the journal's place in American education.

Index